he first brood of Pearly children: we do not know
eir individual names but they are all authentic
early Princes and Princesses. The scene is a
rnival in Kensal Rise Fields.
rca 1914.

THE PEARLIES

THE
PEARLIES
A Social Record

Oh bad luck can't be prevented !
Fortune she smiles or she frowns,
He's best off that's contented
To mix, Sirs, the ups and the downs !

*'Ducklegged Dick' – a coster song
quoted by Henry Mayhew in the 1850s.*

Pearl Binder

1975
JUPITER BOOKS

© 1975 Pearl Binder

First published 1975 by
Jupiter Books (London) Limited
167 Hermitage Road, London N4
SBN 0 904041 182

Set in 11/13pt Monotype Old Style
and printed and bound in Great Britain by
R. J. Acford Ltd, Industrial Estate, Chichester, Sussex

FRONTISPIECE
The first recorded Pearly female dress: Mrs Rose
Matthews, who became the first Pearly Queen of
Hampstead, in her best coster dress with some pearl
button trimming. She wears the white apron of her
coster calling, traditional since the 16th century if
not still earlier. Circa 1890.

Contents

Introduction

This book is about London's East Enders, living north and south of the River Thames, which both unites and divides them. Historically the Tower Hamlets are the oldest part of London and East Enders are deeply attached to their history and to their historic monuments. Their family ties are close and enduring and this is a great source of strength and stability.

Certain basic, often contradictory, cockney characteristics date back beyond the Roman occupation and change not at all: a bubbling street life combined with a deep suspicion of Nosey Parkers; a passion for snacks of fish, preferably shell-fish, eaten standing in the street at all hours of the day or night; a detestation of officers of the law; a protective instinct for verbal mystification; the retention of archaic words and obsolete pronunciation, combined with a relish for coining off-beat new words and phrases; a hunger for dressing-up and showing-off and a talent for making their own finery; a strong democratic outlook together with an equally strong belief in the pecking order; ready charity; skill in organising themselves for anything they want to do; an unquenchable zest for living and a fancy for spectacular funerals.

So precisely do the Pearlies encompass all this that if they had not invented themselves someone would have had to invent them.

London costers are recorded chiefly in English literature on account of their turbulence and noise. Addison in 1711 was writing tetchily in the *Spectator*:

A freeman of London has the Privilege of disturbing a whole street for an hour together with the Twancking of a brass kettle or a Frying Pan.

It is the coster girls who have caught the popular imagination. Nell Gwyn ('pretty witty Nell') selling her oranges outside Drury Lane Theatre; Hogarth's beaming shrimp girl; Eliza Doolittle selling flowers in the rain. Everyone knows what happened to Nell and to Eliza. But what happened to Hogarth's rosy-cheeked shrimp girl, who, unlike Eliza, was a real person? I will venture a guess.

She certainly married a coster, and her coster children begat more coster children. Two centuries later her descendants were still crying shrimps in the streets of London, and some of them surely became Pearly Royalty.

Today, despite the devastation of two world wars and the loss of so many beloved London landmarks, the fifth generation of Pearly children are learning how to wear their Pearly regalia, and being taught their Pearly Royal duties by their nans and great-nans, who have such long and rich memories.

My friend Mrs Beatrice Marriott, born in 1902, elected Festival Pearly Queen of London at the 1951 Festival of Britain, used to sing 'Three Pots a Shilling' with Kate Carney, as a coster child in a chorus of coster children at the old Collins music-hall. She has lived into an age of nuclear fission, electronics and flights to the moon.

The Pearlies could not and did not write down the history they were making. It is time we let them speak for themselves.

SOURCES & ACKNOWLEDGEMENTS

A great deal has been written about the London poor, most of it admonitory or sensational. I have found it more useful to study hospital records, prison regulations and music hall songs ('Any Old Iron', for instance, the popular song of the turn of the century began as a coster street-cry in the 16th century). The poor have their own ways of ensuring that their history shall not be forgotten. Their poignant race-memories are handed down verbally in East End families. Not only what happened, but also what it felt like at the time to those on the receiving end.

Deeply rooted as they are in the life of London, East Enders cherish its history (which is their history) as personal possessions, and it has been ordinary people living east of Aldgate pump who have taught me the London history not to be found in official history books.

Amongst them was my friend John Campbell, an old sailing-ship seaman, who took me in 1930 to a reunion of survivors of the 'Docker's Tanner'* dock strike of 1889. It was held in an old drill-hall in Wapping. We sat at trestle tables with mugs of strong tea and slabs of bread and cheese listening to Ben Tillett and Tom Mann. The dockers were all gaunt and accident-scarred and their talk was peppered with 18th century phrases and still older accents.

It was Daisy Parsons, a respected public figure, an early suffragette who became Mayor of West Ham, who during the election campaign of 1945 took me aside and told me of her experiences as a child skivvy earning her keep when she should have been at school.

Recently, when I played a recording of the old music hall weepie 'My Little Boy' (also known as 'Mother, I Love You') to a Darby and Joan Club in Plaistow, the old ladies (several in their 80s) joined in the moment they heard the opening chords, for they carry these forgotten songs about with them as part of their personalities.

I have quoted extensively in this book from Henry Mayhew's invaluable *London Labour and the London Poor* (1851); Jack London's *People of the Abyss* (1902) has been useful, and George R. Sims' *Living in London* (1903) has yielded several nuggets. Dickens remains though by far the best authority for the London of this period.

Edna Healey has generously shared information about Baroness Burdett-Coutts from her own researches, and Wee Georgie Wood has revealed to me an unforgettable inside view of life in the old music halls. To these two friends my deepest thanks.

Best of all have been the indispensable recordings, already mentioned, taped in 1960, of all the then living Pearlies telling their own stories in their own voices. This, surpassing Mayhew in vivid realism, was master-minded by Marguerite Fawdry, then with the BBC, who also arranged for photographs and drawings and an exhibition to supplement the

* See pages 84 and 86.

tapes. Another series of tapes bringing them up to date was undertaken in 1973 by Jill White, now a BBC archivist.

For Press and film photographs I am indebted to the Hulton Library (now with the BBC), Pathé Gazette Film Library, and Visnews Film Library. John Stanley-Clamp has kindly let us choose from his enormous collection of Pearly photographs, and I must also warmly thank Donald Nicholson, Rosemarie Worters, Kristina Jardell, and S. L. Lewis, who took many Pearly photographs for me at different times.

And, lastly, Mrs Battiscombe for generously allowing me access to her researches into the life of Lord Shaftesbury which have proved most invaluable, and to my secretary, Maxine Hadley, for sustaining me through years of research and revision.

My greatest debt though is to the Pearlies themselves who have remembered and told me so much over many years. I hope this work recalls for them their past and present glories and points to those yet to come!

Self-help and mutual aid: an 18th century engraving
of a street-man collecting victuals and donations for
destitute prisoners.

1.

The
COSTERS

WHO ARE THEY (THE PEARLIES)?

Who exactly are the Pearly Kings and Queens of London? What is their origin? What do they do? How do they live? Are they paid? Are they costers? Are all Pearlies costers? Are all costers Pearlies? Why are Pearlies better known overseas than in England? Are they in decline today?

Briefly – London's Pearly Royalty are a hereditary group of cockneys who, in their spare time, dress up in home-made Pearl-button-jewelled regalia to collect money for charity. Pearlies are unpaid – indeed their charitable excursions and dazzling costume cost them a lot to keep up. Pearlies live as they have always lived – modestly. Sometimes even in penury. Press-photography, and their attendance at overseas British Trade Fairs, have carried their fame all over the world. Though they share with gypsies a love for donkeys and ponies, and a passion for finery and fairs, Pearlies are definitely not gypsies. Not all Pearlies are costers, nor are all costers Pearlies. Costers are much older than Pearlies. It is the costers who have contributed Royalty to the Pearlies. Pearly Royalty only began officially in the 1880s (the *Oxford English Dictionary* first mentions Pearlies by name in 1886); Coster Royalty is rooted in medieval London. Pearly Royalty, though as popular as ever, seems to be in decline today. In their heyday 28 London Boroughs boasted Pearly Royalty and all London wards their Pearly Pride and Pearly helpers, in all probably as many as 400 including Pearly children. Today these have dwindled to about 40.

COCKNEY ROYALTY

The democratic English, particularly the Southern English and most particularly the East Londoners, have always been fascinated by the glamour of titles and regalia. They adore the panoply of Royalty. They have never taken kindly to Protectors or Presidents. Dun-coloured uniformity is anathema to them. They are democrats, but democrats on their own terms. Vertical not horizontal democrats. What they fancy is dustmen Dukes and coster Kings and Queens.

Coster Royalty, so deeply rooted in medieval London, is not an isolated example. Henry the Eighth made himself popular at an archery contest by rewarding the strongest bowman of his bodyguard with the title of 'Earl of Hoxton.* Purely honorary, it entailed no gift of land, money or privilege. Immediately there rose in all the East End hamlets other contestants for 'enoblement' for prowess in archery, resulting in a 'Duke of Whitechapel' and a 'Count of Stepney' etc. thus honoured as outstanding local archers. And these contested 'titles' continued to delight East Londoners until the advance of military technology rendered archery obsolete.

To understand the phenomenon of the London Pearlies it is essential to study the history of the London costers from whom they sprang. Pearly charity took its dynamism from coster charity. The breezy extrovert Pearly way of life is the mirror image of the breezy extrovert coster way of life. The Pearlies did not burst upon the London scene until the 1880s but their advent had been prepared for by many centuries of coster tradition. *The Pearlies*, it is true to say, *are the final flowering of Coster culture.*

COSTER HISTORY

To understand the Pearly phenomenon it is vital to understand the peculiar character of the London poor, that is the London poor *as they see themselves.* We must go right back into London history. The Pearlies began in the 1880's and a mere century may well complete their extraordinary cycle. But cockney-coster regional Royalty, though known to few, dates back at least to the Middle Ages.

* Surely the origin of the name 'kingsman' which costers have given to their silk kerchief.

The vinegar-vendor – a 17th century London coster
with his donkey.

There were hucksters crying their wares in the streets of London from
very early times. The word 'coster' is derived from 'costard' ('custard'?),
a large cooking apple. Monger simply means *vendor*. The word 'coster'
appears in an English MS as early as 1292. By Shakespeare's time
costers were so much part of the London street scene that they are
mentioned by name in several plays.

> Virtue is of so little regard in these coster-monger
> times that true valour is turned bear-herd.
>   Shakespeare's *Henry V*

The noise of costermongers crying their wares was seized upon by Ben
Jonson (*Epicene*, 1609), whose fastidious Morose demanded that the
fishwives and orange-women should abate their clamour because he
'cannot endure a costermonger. He swoons if he hears one.'

In Ford's *Suns's Darling* we find:

Upon my life he means to turn coster-monger, and is projecting how to
forestall the market. I shall cry pippins rarely.

In Beaumont and Fletcher traditional coster back-chat is immortalised:

> Pray sister do not laugh; you'll anger him
> And then he'll rail like a rude coster-monger.

In the 18th century Doctor Johnson spells it 'costard-monger' describing the word in his dictionary as a seller of apples 'round and bulky like the head'.

Shouting or 'crying' his wares in the streets has always been the coster's method of attracting customers. The London coster has always been noisy and assertive, as he needed to be to make a living in the competitive crowded streets. In the 19th century he beat a hand-drum or tin when his voice failed.

The late John Marriott the third (Festival Pearly King of London, and Leader of the London Pearlies) gave me the following version of the origin of Pearly Monarchy –

THE FIRST COSTER KINGS

The highly competitive trade of costermongering, dependent on individual effort and personality, always attracted the attention of bullies who tried to force costermongers from their good pitches in order to seize these pitches for themselves. This led to fights and trouble with authority. As the costers had no licence (being merely permitted to ply their trade at the discretion of the local authorities) the costers could not invoke the law to protect themselves. They therefore met together in secret in each borough to choose one outstanding coster from amongst themselves as their representative to stand up for them physically against the bullies, and when there was trouble with the local authority to speak up for them.

Such a man would be chosen for his physical strength and courage, his quality of leadership, loyalty to his coster mates, quick-wittedness, and strong personality. As with the archery nobility, he was elected their local 'King'.

The costers in their own secretive-communal way had started something, and in traditional English fashion so it continued. Each regional coster King had his Queen, and these had their 'royal' children. As with royal royals these monarchies were hereditary – the heir to the coster local monarchy being duly invested with the powers and duties of his royal father when he inherited his title.

A 17th century London oyster-vendor with an early coster hand-barrow.

To some extent shielded by their elected local kings, the costers continued to cry their wares from their unlicensed pitches, and the bullies continued their aggressive attacks to dislodge them.

COSTERS & THEIR PITCHES

Not only were fights common between costers and bullies for the possession of pitches, but also fights between costers and police for 'making an affray', or for using any pitch at all. This unsatisfactory situation was inevitable because the costers had no licence to be selling their wares on the streets. They were there on sufferance.

Even today the question of licensing costers is very tricky. Local authorities are obliged to keep their thoroughfares open to traffic. Crowds may not gather. There must be no affray. Local authorities hate giving licences for street trading which encourages crowds to gather. Yet the only way to keep law and order is to grant licences and so bring costers within reach and protection of the law. There have always been more costers than accommodation – more costers who want stalls than markets can hold, more street sellers than authority can tolerate. This impossible situation has still never been properly cleared up. The present

Pearly Prince Consort of Camden, George Matthew Smith, told me how difficult it was in the 1930s for him to push his laden vegetable barrow along Camden High Street with his hips, to keep in motion whilst he wrapped up bags of tomatoes and gave change on the move under the vigilant eyes of the local constable. In London streets today it is still illegal to keep a barrow standing still without a licence. Stalls in street markets are now licensed and taxed but when every sunny summer day may bring out a surge of strawberries on handcarts – every power strike a flood of barrows touting candles – how can these be controlled?

In the 19th century only relatively few costers could hope for a regular stall in a regular market. Henry Mayhew calculated an average of fourteen street stalls to a mile. This was in 1851. Even when such licences were granted to a very few street vendors, the rest of the costers still had to be kept on the move. If a coster 'stood still' to make a sale, even momentarily, that coster was liable to arrest and imprisonment for 'loitering'. For centuries this impossible situation was the chief cause of the hatred and frequent street-fights between costers and local authority represented by 'police', whom costers regarded as their chief enemy. It was the ambiguous law which the costers resented, and it was as the instrument of the law that the police roused their bitterest hatred.

The coster 'King's' job was to stand up to the police, to stand up in court and speak up for the costers, and if necessary to go bravely to prison. He represented to the costers their own solidarity and concern for each other. Though the law was against them, though the small shop-keepers (rate-payers who detested the costers who paid no rates because they had no property) were against them, and in general *they* were against them, *their King was for them.*

COSTERS & THEIR TASK

Yet, as the costers well knew, the authorities could not manage to feed the London poor without the help of the costers. 'What would the Duke of Bedford's market in Covent Garden be without the likes of us?', a coster spokesman declared at Henry Mayhew's Costers' Meeting in Holborn in 1850. The millions of poor Londoners had somehow to be supplied on the spot where they lived with the cheapest victuals in the smallest retail quantities.

Shops were too dear and did not encourage customers from the poorest class who might frighten off better customers. The difficulties and cost of transport were such that only the costers, with their willingness to work inhuman hours and retail food they had pushed miles from the morning central market, and would continue to push till nightfall through the alleys and courts where their customers lived, could tackle this immense task. London transport was not up to it. Nor were the small shops, so tiny was the margin of profit involved, so great the risk of failure and bankruptcy. ·

Poor Londoners hardly budged from their native alleys and courts. The costers carried their food to them, in farthing's worths.

The costers knew they were indispensable, and this whetted their fury against the police for interfering with them on their rounds. Behind it all lurked the Government's fear of street-crowds giving rise to turbulence. And, from Cromwell's time, the middle-class British protestant attitude towards poverty – that such a state was sinful and that those who were poor had only themselves to blame. It is an attitude which the costers wryly recognised in their dealings with the police and with authority and which was later to spur the Pearlies in their charitable efforts to do something human to make amends.

COSTERS & LORD SHAFTESBURY

John Marriott assured me that it was Lord Shaftesbury who succeeded in putting an end to the fighting between costers and police, by promising to get London costers their licence in return for their promise to stop fighting the police.*

Lord Shaftesbury was, according to his religious lights and the times he lived in, a friend to the poor, an indefatigable fighter for his bills on their behalf in the House of Lords. Amongst other charitable institutions he founded were the Costermongers' Mission and the Band of the Costermongers Temperance Society which played the 'March from Saul' at his funeral in Westminster Abbey on 8 October 1885. Also represented were the Shoeblacks Brigade, the Ragged Schools, the London City Mission etc.

That the hard-drinking, godless, belligerent London costers described by Mayhew in 1851 should in one generation have seen the light, transforming themselves, to please Lord Shaftesbury, into saintly capdoffers and teetotal Sunday-school attenders does not, on the face of it, carry much conviction. But the costers, like all poor Londoners,

*In fact there is no record in *Hansard* of Lord Shaftesbury speaking on behalf of the costers in Parliament. London metropolitan Borough Councils eventually took over the control of street trading in their respective areas.

"THE EARL'S BARROW."

"I am a costermonger."—Vide Lord Shaftesbury's Speech at Golden Lane.

recognise their friends and have never lacked a sense of obligation to those who have tried to help them. Amongst the swollen ranks of London costers it must be remembered were unemployed artisans from the shut-down factories and mills of the north of England. These men tended to be chapel-goers and teetotallers. They certainly would have welcomed Lord Shaftesbury's well-meaning institutions. The 'March from Saul' would be just up their street, for they were devoted to religious music and brass bands.

Lord Shaftesbury undoubtedly liked the London costers. It is on record that he took the trouble to have a special coster's handbarrow made, painted with his own coat of arms, which he lent out free of charge to poor costers who could not afford to rent a barrow of their own. It is also on record that in recognition of his interest in them the costers subscribed to the purchase of a donkey which they gave to him as a gift. This donkey was never used to draw a cart but lived out a life of ease on Lord Shaftesbury's estates.

Even so, Lord Shaftesbury's efforts did not put an end to the bitter warfare between costers and police. To this day there is no love lost between them.

ANOTHER KINGSHIP THEORY

There is also another theory which must be noted concerning coster Kingship. A. L. Lloyd (the musicologist and folklore authority) suggests the following origin. He believes that the costers' continual struggle against the police (representing authority) reflected a much older tradition, and that the coster 'Monarch' was really the ancient 'Lord of Misrule', the blowhole supervisor of annual permitted disorder. This takes Kingship even further back in English history.

LITERATURE ABOUT COSTERS

It is to be expected that so venerable a group of open-air traders as the London costers should have developed their own total way of life, places of residence, partialities and aversions, superstitions and ceremonies, secret language, race-memories, and above all their own way of looking after their own people.

We have several sources of detailed information about London costers in the 19th century. There is Charles Dickens (1812–1870). There is Henry Mayhew's encyclopaedic *London Labour and the London Poor* (published in 1851), Jack London's *People of the Abyss* (published in 1902) and George R. Sims' *Living in London* (published in 1903).

Mayhew was pious, efficient and good-hearted. Sims was sentimental. Jack London was too American to understand the cockney character. Only Dickens, wanderer in the streets of London at all times, really understood the cockney characters of his age. His own impoverished childhood gave him this understanding.

Mayhew, invaluable for his lively descriptions and painstaking statistics, was as much shocked by the costers' godlessness and contempt for the marriage ceremony as he was by their poverty and insecurity. They did not take the holy name seriously at all. 'Jesus Christ? Our Redeemer? Well I only wish I could redeem my Sunday togs from my Uncle's'!

Mayhew always brought religion into his questions to costers on their way of life. They told him that they had no time for Christian preachers and that tracts 'Gives us the 'orrors'.* 'There's no costermongers ever go to church except the rogues of them that wants to appear good', he reports a woman of 38 saying who kept a little fruit stall in Marylebone.

In the fifty years between Mayhew's reporting and the accounts of G. R. Sims and Jack London, the already desperate economic situation of the London costers had worsened. The contrasts between rich and poor had widened still further. The East End was even more crowded, traffic more congested, prisons more choked with miscreants. The Pearlies had arrived and delighted cockney London but neither Sims nor Jack London mentions them. Jack London painted the gloomiest picture of East End life, exact in its limited observation yet lacking in comprehension of the cockney character and its essential resilient gaiety. London wrote of the dockland poor with horror. Though he himself was of working-class origin and an alcoholic, he could not identify with the London poor, nor understand their passion for alcohol. American, he could never understand why poor Londoners did not get out of their misery by emigrating to California.

To learn about them 'from the inside' he went to the trouble of buying second-hand clothes, renting the cheapest lodgings and pretending he was a sailor looking for a ship. But the doss-house cockneys he met knew he was not one of themselves – and no doubt told him (as cockneys delight in telling) only what he wanted to hear.

The lurid image of 19th century East End London, so starkly contrasted with the ostentatious luxury and wealth of West End London, fascinated America and the Continent and an endless stream of private observers and commissioned graphic artists, amongst them Doré and Gavarni, came or were sent from overseas to have a good look. The cockney being what he is, no doubt played up to what was expected of him.

The most authentic pictures we have of the London poor in the last quarter of the 19th century are Phil May's ink drawings. Phil May (addicted to alcohol and betting like most cockneys) saw and drew what he saw truly. Perhaps because, so English himself and with a straitened childhood, he identified with the mean streets and the cheerfulness bred by desperation. He was an observant artist first and foremost and this further enriched his appreciation.

---

*A census taken in 1851 revealed that out of 18 million English people only 7 million (much less than 50%) attended any kind of church at all.

The 16th century London costers crying their wares. The town-crier is in the centre.

MAYHEW'S COSTERS (1851)

When Mayhew was compiling his survey Great Britain was at the height of her power as a great Empire whose wealth, from industrial development at home and vast possessions and markets overseas, had established her firmly as the richest and strongest nation in the world.

Social classes in England had never been tighter. Law-breakers were punished swiftly and with the utmost severity. Even minor theft could incur transportation. Robert Peel wrote to Sydney Smith that it was extremely difficult to make prison conditions and prison diet more unpleasant than anything the 'criminal classes' experienced outside and so maintain a 'salutory terror'. The treadmill was not abolished in English jails until 1901. It had been used to supply mechanical power for the prison by human effort. It necessitated so severe an effort that

21

The costers through foreign eyes: the bustle of Covent Garden Market. Sketches by G. Scharf dating from the early 1820s.

only the strongest prisoners were medically passed as fit for treadmill service, and then only for four minutes at a stretch with one minute's rest.

In Mayhew's time masses of poor Londoners (their numbers continually augmented by unemployed mill and factory workers and evicted smallholders who took to the road and walked to London) scrambled to earn their living by any kind of job – petty huckstering, sweeping street crossings, dung gathering. (Anything except direct begging which was illegal.)

Though it was the most arduous and uncertain trade of all, costermongering ranked highest amongst the street hucksters and attracted more outsiders. For London in 1851 Mayhew gives the figure of 30,000 costers, including their women and children who also worked as costers. There had been a census taken in 1841 which gave their number as only 2,045, a figure which Mayhew rightly dismissed as ridiculous because not one coster in 20 had bothered to fill in the census returns. For two excellent reasons – first they were unable to read and write and second they deeply distrusted the authorities. Mayhew's estimated 30,000 costers increased rapidly year by year as unemployed servants, out-of-work farm-hands, even actors out of a job 'took to the coster's barrow'. During the Irish famine of the 1840s the number of Irish costers in London had doubled. The trade of costermongering, already working on so delicate and tiny a margin of viability, was grossly overcrowded. When even experienced London costers, born and brought up to the trade, could be ruined in a matter of days, so little was their margin, it

LITTLE MOTHERS.

was inevitable that the newcomers should almost all fail and fall into destitution. Costers had no guild, no craft organisation, no way of controlling the numbers of costers and would-be costers. The work was seasonal, susceptible to every economic tremor, and totally dependent on the weather. Three wet Saturdays spelt ruin to countless costers.

Yet, Mayhew records, they never turned in anger against the newcomers competing against them for their customers. Rather they expressed pity for them knowing what they were in for.

'They go to market with fear, and don't know how to venture a bargain if one offers', a coster told Mayhew. 'Some of these poor fellows lose every penny. They're middle-aged when they begin costering. We pity them. It's awful to see them for they don't set about it right. Besides there's too many before they start. They don't find a living. It's only another way of starving.'

COSTERS & MONEYLENDERS

Illiterate and unorganised, the costers were no match for the moneylenders who held them in a remorseless grip. It was not improvidence but having no capital of their own to start with which held the costers down. Those few, those very few, who did not drink and were non-givers when 'the basin went round' (to help fellow costers in trouble), could exceptionally struggle their way up into becoming a 'settled man', owner of a coalshed or small store selling oysters (then very cheap) and ginger beer. Some usurers had even started like this, but at the expense of the openhearted quality of life and openhandedness the costers valued in themselves. Servant-girls, too prudent to settle for the insecurity of a coster's life, would agree to 'marrying a coalshed'. But the sweated factory girls, who earned no more than 4/6 for a long week's labour, all dreamed of marrying a coster, whom they regarded as a real man.

Costers, beyond their immediate transactions, had no understanding of money, investment, interest. They had the same instinctive aversion to paper money one finds in Australian desert aborigines, and no doubt for the same reason: being mere paper and handled out of doors, it might blow away. Costers when wronged in business deals never took their grievances to Court, distrusting law and lawyers as much as they distrusted Police. They preferred to fight it out physically on the spot.

Even those costers who by a stroke of luck or a run of fine weather plus fortunate stock-buying, had acquired a little money, did not understand how beneficial for them it would be to buy, instead of hire, the implements of their trade. Their bank was their pocket. Mayhew gives these figures:

The hire of a barrow cost 3d per day or 1/- per week in winter, 4d per day or 1/6 per week in summer, and 6d on Saturdays.*

A good new barrow could be purchased for £2/12/-, a good slightly used barrow could be purchased in the autumn or winter for as little as 30/- or even less. Over a period of eight years a coster would pay £26 or more (and still own nothing) for the rental of a barrow he could have bought in the first place (had he the small capital and the understanding) for 26/-.

Donkeycarts were rarely hired, but bought outright, £3/10/- being the average price. Hiring cost 2/1 or 2/6 a week. Harnesses costing £2/10/- new were usually bought second-hand for 2/6 to 20/- depending on their condition. The donkeys had to be bought at a price varying from £1 to £3. If hired from a coster the fee was 2/6 to 3/- per week. There were also a few ponies which could be bought at prices ranging from £3 to £13, but there were always at least six times as many donkeys in use as ponies. It must be remembered that only the cream of the coster profession were donkey-owning.

Other tools of their trade used by costers were shallow (baskets) and scales. Shallows were mostly used by girl costers and cost one shilling to 1/6 to buy, but could be hired, when this capital investment was lacking, for a penny a day. A pewter quart-pot, for measuring onions etc. cost but 2/- when bought and could also be hired at 2d per day. Scales cost 2d per day to hire and their weights 1d per day.

Worse than the weather, which could ruin them, worse than the police who could arrest them in the street, were the moneylenders. Everything the costers needed for their work: barrow, shallow, scales and stockmoney, had to be rented from the moneylenders at grossly usurious rates of interest. *20% per week was usual.* 20% per week is 1040% per annum. (This at a time when 10% per annum, the standard rate of interest, was regarded by London banks as a just return on capital invested.) Failure to pay up promptly (capital plus interest) was punished by the moneylender driving the coster out of business by refusing a further loan and making sure that no other moneylender would ever afterwards loan him money.

It was stockmoney and the rate of interest charged for its loan which caused the costers their greatest anxiety. The usual stockmoney loan

*All prices and costs are given in pre-decimilisation pounds, shillings and pence.

The costers through foreign eyes: 'Le gin' from Gavarni's collection of lithographs, *Les Anglais chex eux*, published in 1845.

was 2/- up to 10/- for one day's business. The usurers' charges were 2d per day on a loan of 2/6, 3d per day on a loan of 5/-, 6d per day on a loan of 10/- and 1/- a day on a loan of £1.

The coster had to borrow his stockmoney daily and repay it with the added interest that same night. Mayhew mentions the coster who was destroyed by taking on himself a debt of ten shillings which (with the interest added) he sweated for ten months to repay at the rate of one shilling and sixpence a week. He dared not default, however bad the weather. In fact the coster repaid 60/- for the loan of 10/-.'And that', he told Mayhew, 'really did me up'.

'I paid 2/- a week for a whole year' another coster informed Mayhew (or £5/4/-), 'for the use of that £1 I borrowed, and then I was liable to repay the £1'. Mayhew calculated that one usurer who had a capital of £150 floating in loans to costermongers, at the rate of interest of 2/- per week per £1, would have accumulated £390 in a season of only 26 weeks. Usurers loaned money all the 52 weeks of each year.

Costers were obliged to borrow small sums to catch the important days when sales might be expected (Wednesdays and Fridays, and especially Saturdays). They were in no position to haggle and therefore totally at the mercy of the usurers. Often a loan was solicited just for one day, and that a Saturday, when as much as 2/6 would be charged for a loan of 5/-, both capital and interest having to be repaid without fail that same night.

Beershop owners (not regular moneylenders) also lent money to the costers but they expected the borrower to buy a lot of beer in their establishment.

'In the depth of last winter', one coster confided in Mayhew, 'I borrowed 5/-. The beershop keeper wouldn't lend. He'll rather lend to men doing well and drinking. But I borrowed it at 6d a day interest and that 6d a day I paid for exactly four weeks, Sundays and all, and that was 15/- in thirty days for the use of 5/-. I was half starving all the time and then I had a slice of luck and paid the 5/- back slap and got out of it.'

He considered himself lucky.

COSTER SEASONS

The costers' trade was seasonal, varying in stock and earnings with the time of year. In the winter time (ushered in by the Lord Mayor's annual banquet) they sold sprats and herrings, the most popular 'relishes' of poor Londoners. They hoped to clear 8/- a week, but could exceptionally, with luck and good management, even make as much as £2. March was always a dreadful month, a coster's barrow might be idle for a week at a time but its hire still had to be paid.

At the end of March the appearance of early Spring flowers 'all a'growing and a'blowing' enabled the costers (or their girls, because flowers were often sold from shallows) to clear at least 5/- a week.

Gustav Dore's engraving of 'Outcasts under the Bridges' from 1871 conveys the squalor and oppression of 19th century life in the East End of London.

Customers were cheered at the hope of sun and warmth ahead.

In May fresh fish came on the market. Also rooted flowers such as wall-flowers and stocks (for window boxes). 10/- to 12/- might be earned.

June brought new potatoes and peas, also beans. An extra 1/- could be earned (11/- a week, and with luck even as much as £1).

July was the season for cherries, a tricky stock (4/- to 8/- a day if the weather was good). No fish would be available, but all the summer fruits, strawberries, raspberries, currants and gooseberries. 5/- to 6/- a day with luck and up to 30/- or even 36/- a week. But though everyone loved the summer, fresh soft fruit was always an anxiety for the coster. Working people did not greatly care for soft fruit. They were unused to it. And the cholera epidemics frightened off those who did care for it. In Mayhew's time owing to the cholera epidemic of 1849 which was believed to be spread by fruit and vegetables, costers were doing less business and at smaller profit. By the end of the century this situation had worsened.

September brought apples and a hope of 2/6 a day profit.

October brought fish again. Oysters being a very popular working-class food (eaten in ones or twos) meant a gain of 1/- a day.

In November fish and vegetables were both available. 1/- to 2/- a day could be hoped for, more if sprats were already in.

December was the month for fish with 1/- to 1/6 profit a day and with the extra hope of selling a few oranges and lemons near Christmas.

In Christmas week a lively coster could make 3/- to 4/- a day.

COSTERS & THE SUNDAY DINNER

The nutrition of the costers, like that of the very poor for whom they catered, was scanty and ill-balanced. Chiefly it consisted of bread and tea, a few vegetables and, when in the cheap flush of season, occasionally a little fruit. Sprats, in season, were the most popular of all foodstuffs. At a penny per pound sprats went further and were considered tastier than herrings. Sprats were regarded as a blessing and credited with the power of keeping out the cold. The very poorest never saw meat. Those slightly higher in the social scale hoped for a meat dinner on Sundays.

It was this Sunday dinner, with its accompanying vegetables (and in time of prosperity even a pudding as well) which gave the costers their best selling period of the week, Saturday night – till all hours.

This traditional British Sunday midday dinner (a roast with vegetables) has always been the mainstay of British working class life. Upon it all pride depends. Without it decency and self-respect vanish. Charles Chaplin recalls, in his autobiography, the terrible Sunday of humiliation when he was a child in Lambeth and there was no money to afford this ritual Sunday dinner, and how his mother begged him and his brother Sydney to clatter their knives and forks on their empty plates so that the neighbours should think they were eating their Sunday dinner and not starving.

THE COSTER'S DAY

In the mid-19th century costers rose at 4 a.m. and hurried to the central markets with their barrows and shallows. There, with anxious consideration, they expended their stockmoney (borrowed from the moneylender the previous night at the public house). Then, the day's stock safely bought in, they would (if they could spare the money) buy themselves a cup of coffee and a slice of bread for breakfast. For the rest of the day any other food would be bought and devoured on the street on the move from a pie-man or hot-potato vendor. Not till his long day ended was a coster free to go back to his pub and cook himself a scrappy meal ('block ornaments'* if he had had a good day) on the communal fire. He then had to borrow the necessary stockmoney for the following day's business *after* he had paid the moneylender back the amount loaned plus interest for the day which was finishing.

Every morning except Sunday (unless he had done exceptionally badly during the week and would also have to turn out for the Sunday morning market) the coster having made his purchase in the market would carefully load his barrow. This skilled operation was governed by rules not unlike those regulating the loading of a cargo ship. A loaded barrow weighed thirteen hundredweights, and unless the weight was properly distributed the barrow could not be pushed at all. Also the wares had to look appetising to tempt customers. Some barrows were enlivened by a gaily coloured flag at each corner.

Then, aided by the beating of a stick against a tin box, the coster began his twelve to fourteen hour trudge round and round the courts and alleys of his beat – treading out at least ten miles every day. So long as his voice lasted the coster cried for himself, but it soon gave out. Then he had to take on a boy apprentice to cry for him.

'Here pertaters! Kearots and Turnips! Fine Brocelo-o!'

*'Block ornaments' — the cheapest trimmings cut away from butcher's meat portions.

'An aypenny a lot ing-uns*!'

'Penny a lot, fine russets!'

'Twopence a 'pahnd', GRAPES!'

Back and forth the coster pushed his barrow over the cobbles and paving-stones of his beat – alert to coax any possible customer – always ready, if she hesitated, to beguile her with cockney wit so that the simple transaction became a pleasure to her. Always alert too, that there was no policeman in sight when he stopped to weigh the purchase and take his payment. If he were caught stopping he could instantly be arrested for 'loitering'.

In the smallest amounts the coster gradually disposed of his day's stock, continually tramping his beat 'rahnd the 'ahses', back and forth over the same cobblestones. At the end of his day, if any of his stock were left over, he made a final tour, selling it off very cheap to the very poorest who could never afford anything but left-overs. He made nothing probably was himself out of pocket on these final sales, which would take him till 11 p.m.

Some days, even when it did not rain, went badly. There was no money about, hardly any customers. Or had he invested unwisely in stock no-one cared to buy? Every coster knew such days. Or, taking a great chance, he might push his barrow far afield 'all rahnd the country' perhaps as far as Greenwich or Richmond. Farm labourers, curiously enough, rarely knew fresh vegetables and were always eager to buy a few sprats. But there were expenses for the coster going so far afield. There were toll gates with a special charge on push-barrows. Sometimes after all his trouble, fatigue and expense, no-one bought. Unlucky costers, crying that they were 'ruined', sometimes threw away their fading stock over the nearest hedge in despair, rather than push the laden barrow back again.

The uncle of an old lady still alive in West Ham, as a young man at the turn of the century, pushed a handcart (laden with hand-brooms he had made himself) all the way from East London to Brighton, where he sold very few, and pushed them all the way back to the East End again in thirty-six hours.

Wet days, particularly wet Saturdays, and worst of all a succession of wet Saturdays, spelled total disaster for costers. Those who had risen to the eminence of donkey-carts could not take out their donkeys. The rest, with push-carts or shallows prepared to brave the rain but their

*Onions.

32

customers had vanished. Poor people with only one garment and no fire nor umbrella dared not venture out in bad weather. The costers took themselves to their pub, where in despair they gambled all day, even gambling away their stockmoney. Their women would take their shallows round the pubs, but with everyone selling and no-one buying there was no custom. On wet days the costers drank heavily.

COSTERS & DRINKING

The drinking habits of the costers, which so distressed Mayhew, did not abate with the passage of time and were as bad, if not worse, by 1900. One of the chief reasons for the heavy drinking of the English poor, which all foreign visitors commented upon, was that drink was so cheap, so easily available and took away the appetite. It was much cheaper to drink than to eat. Beer was the costers' usual drink. But a vast amount of gin was also drunk in the pubs. And the gin-palaces were brightly illuminated, gorgeous to sit in, and warm. 'Every two or three steps a ginshop', commented Nathaniel Hawthorne (stationed in England as an American consul). It was his opinion that the poor in England could only maintain their animal heat by means of alcohol, without which the harsh climate would destroy them.

'No-one drinks water here' complained Joachim Miller, visiting London's East End in 1870. And for an excellent reason, the water supply being so impure that typhoid and cholera epidemics were frequent. Even the highest in the land were not immune. The Prince Consort himself, it was believed, died from typhoid. Serious social reformers, trying to wean the poor from intemperance, set up a chain of 'hygenic' public drinking fountains in poor districts, with a chained metal cup, and engraved inscription inviting passers-by to partake of 'God's pure crystal stream'. But the Londoners remained deeply suspicious of water.

COSTERS' LODGINGS

Costers hardly saw their rented room, since they rose at 4 a.m. each day only returning to it after midnight. Their working lives, courtship, fights, quarrels, friendships, all took place in the street. The streets were their home, and they were deeply attached to the grimy London alleys where they trod out their lives, expressing pity for the poor factory workers who laboured indoors, whilst costers were enjoying what they insisted on believing to be the fresh air in the streets (the air of the

East End was then thickly polluted by coal-smoke, industrial waste and nauseous gases). The streets were the costers' home, and the pub was his club. Often the same landlord owned both the mean courts and alleys and the public house which stood at the corner. Nothing was spent by the landlord to make the coster's rented room habitable. Roofs were never mended, paintwork was never renewed, floorboards were allowed to rot and the furniture provided by the landlord was decrepit and inadequate. Quite late in the 19th century landlords were still building rows of mean houses in the East End of London with no running water nor any form of WC sanitation.

COSTERS' PUBS

The intention was to encourage the tenants to seek refuge from their dismal rooms and spend their money in the public houses. In these gorgeous palaces, so typical of East London in the last quarter of the 19th century, no expense was spared to make them luxurious, romantic, deeply comfortable and a delight to the eye.* Much marble, rich patterned tiles, shining mahogany, glittering brass-work, ornate gilded sandblasted mirrors (which looked Venetian but in point of fact were made to order in the nearby London glass-works in Wapping); moulded fancy Lincrusta ceilings and friezes – an abundance of grandiose double lettering, sprouting flowers and foliage, sumptuously gilded and ornamented. Costers, like other illiterates, were deeply attached to this fancy lettering. Sometimes there would be a parrot in a fine brass cage.

These gorgeous public houses were warm, clean, and brightly lit. Here it was that the costers drank their beer, gambled (illegally), borrowed their stock-money for the next day from their moneylender, paid their rent, and enjoyed free concerts. Anyone could get up to sing or do a turn and then take a collection. It was one way of making up for a disastrous day outside in the streets. But these turns had to be good. The coster audience was highly critical. There would very often be a basin going round to help a coster in trouble.

COSTERS & GAMBLING

In the beershops in wet weather, gambling was continual. The games were cribbage, all-fives and put. Whist was considered tedious and slow, unworthy of the coster spirit. The costers played for beer and bets

*As early as 1836 Charles Dickens declared that the London pubs were displaying 'An inordinate love of plate glass and a passion for gas-lights and gilding, – stone balustrades, rosewood fittings, immense lamps and illuminated clocks at the corner of every street'.

ranged from one penny to five shillings. The landlord usually supplied the cards, but sporting costers carried a couple of packs in their pockets for use at any free moment. Mayhew observed that these costers, illiterate and with no knowledge of arithmetic, were amazingly quick and skilful in card-game calculation.

Drinking was a distraction. In Mayhew's time it was gambling which provided the chief emotional outlet for the costers. Coster children began gambling for buttons almost as soon as they could walk. Little coster boys would even pluck off their trouser buttons when losing, so that when defeated they would be obliged to retire holding up their trousers with their hands. From the age of thirteen or fourteen a coster lad graduated from buttons to coins. 'Er pu' ('three up') was their favourite game.

Their Sunday morning gambling sites were the Fields by Kings Cross, near the Mint, by St George's-in-the-Fields, Blackfriar's Road, Bethnal Green and Marylebone, but especially the shingled beach south of the Thames between Lambeth and Chelsea. Gambling was illegal. And that added spice to their sport. Hidden behind moored barges they hoped to escape the eye of the prying policeman. But they also posted a look-out who was paid a trifle for his pains. If he spied a policeman he cried out in coster reversed slang 'Cool! Esclop!' so that by the time the policeman arrived the lads would be chatting, hands in pockets, with innocent faces.

Gambling went on for hours on end as the tensions built up, with shouts of:

'Sixpence Red wins! Bet you a gen!'

'Sixpence he loses! I'll bet you a rouf genap!'

'No use! Luck's set in 'im. E'd much a thahsand!'

'You'll win the shine-rag, Jo!'

These lads were enacting the daily gamble that was to be their life. They gambled whilst waiting for the morning market to open, and they tossed the pie-man for their dinner. Someone had to win. Someone had to lose. When, half a century later, the Pearlies organized themselves, they chose as their motto 'You Never Know'.

One coster lad, Mayhew reports, arrived at the gambling site in bitter weather dressed in good clothes and a warm overcoat. Losing, he gambled away his overcoat, his warm suit, his 'kingsman'* – earnings of many weeks' toil. And finally he gambled away his precious stock-

*Kerchief.

money for the next day too.

An old coster gambling at the races with an astute thimble-rigger lost, in less than an hour, his stock, his pony, his cart and his greatcoat. He returned home on foot, carrying his boy on his back as a gesture of bravado. Case histories like these were recounted by the East End Missions with horror. They were recounted by the costers as instances of the working of fate. The great thing was to pick yourself up cheerfully and start all over again without moaning. Style and panache were what the costers admired, both in life and in death.

Those who had lost everything hung round watching the betting and offering advice. A losing youth adopted every device to change his luck, practising throwing techniques before his real toss, changing his place in the circle, and turning his waistcoat inside out (as the 18th century gamblers did in the aristocratic gambling clubs in the West End).

When the weather was so wet that the coins stuck to the ground, the coster youths would find themselves a refuge under some railway arch or join their elders at the beershop and gamble there.

Girls and women rarely gambled, not from prudence nor virtue, but because, they declared, it gave them 'no excitement'. Sunday morning was the time when they cleaned up their room, mended their clothes and attended to the family chores. There was also the precious Sunday dinner, if they could afford one, to be cooked on a handful of small coals.

COSTERS & SELF DEFENCE

Gambling was not confined to cards and coin-tossing. Skittles was a popular sport and an excuse for the laying of bets. So were rat-fights, dog-fights, pigeon-shooting and pigeon-racing. The costers were devoted to birds and reared pigeons successfully in lath cages on the roofs of their tenements. (Pigeons are still reared in this way today in the narrow streets round Leather Lane, Holborn, the famous coster street market.) Boxing, and all physical sport within their means, was popular with costers, and yet another source of betting. Learning to fight was regarded as essential to a boy's upbringing, cowardice in any form being despised. Even girls had to learn how to 'work their fists well'.

Any coster, male or female, of whatever age, if struck was morally obliged to return the blow. A quarrel between men, between boys, between women, between girls could only be resolved in a set fight, and no self-respecting coster would have thought of stopping such a fight, lest it 'cause bad blood for life'. The fight over, the victor acclaimed, the loser respected if he had put up a good fight, hands were shaken and the affair was regarded as over and forgotten.

If it sounds like *Tom Brown's Schooldays* there was one basic difference. The costers were consciously training themselves for battle against their common enemy, the police. The coster expression of admiration for prowess was simply:

'He could muzzle half-a-dozen coppers before breakfast.'

'To serve out a policeman is the bravest act by which a coster can distinguish himself', reported Mayhew. 'Some lads have been imprisoned upwards of a dozen times for this offence, and are consequently looked upon by their companions as martyrs.'

The police were blamed for all the evils from which the costers suffered. They were the symbol of the oppressive Establishment, which, costers felt, hounded them, cheated them, allowed them no say in the making of the laws of the country which pressed them so hard. They could see for themselves that the police were obsequious to those who had money and in precise proportion to their wealth. The police always seemed to them to be against the poor, of whom the costers considered themselves the natural champions.

LIVING CONDITIONS

Examples from Mayhew:

In one room three children without parents (a girl of 15, her brother of 13 who worked as a costermonger's boy, and a younger girl of 11) paid two shillings a week for their furnished room, all three sleeping in the one bed. This room was sublet to them by their Irish 'landlord' who himself took his cut. The two girls sold flowers in the streets. The older girl said they tried to keep respectable and 'never troubled the Parish'. They tried to make sixpence a day on which they could survive on a diet of bread and tea with an occasional herring for supper. When times were bad they had to go to the dolly-shop (illegal pawnbrokers) which charged twopence a week for the loan of a shilling. Their brother earned 1/6 a week from his coster master who occasionally also gave him a meal. The girls lived on two shillings a week, the rest all going for rent.

An old woman, who sold pigs' trotters for a living, paid one shilling and fourpence for the room she rented, which she shared. Another old woman, also a pigs' trotter seller, paid one shilling a week for still worse accommodation which she shared with her crippled son.

The poorest Londoners, Mayhew observed, invented jobs which

'The Wallflower Girl' – a young coster child selling
flowers in the street in the 1850s.

needed no, or almost no, outlay. There were groundsel-sellers (for feeding linnets), brace-makers (one shilling for making four dozen). There were vendors of catsmeat and dogsmeat and chickweed, all of whom thought themselves lucky if they could get a room for their family at 2/- and keep 'respectable' by not sinking right to the bottom of the social scale. At the bottom were the terrible 'Paddington-Kens' where lodged thieves, vagabonds and prostitutes; Westminster, a stone's throw from the Houses of Parliament, and Holborn, were similarly notorious.

COSTERS & THE WORKHOUSE

As costers ranked highest in the street-vendors' hierarchy, so when they failed ('cracked up', 'cursed', and 'ruined'), their descent was more agonising. A run of bad luck, a run of bad weather, cholera, disastrous gambling, could unloose a coster's grip on a living. He lost his gambler's nerve as he pawned everything he had left, and lost his pride. The final act of despair for a coster was to be forced to apply to the Union (work-house or 'Big House') for charity. One reason why English costers dis-liked Irish costers was because Irish costers were immune to shame in applying to the Parish for relief.* Costers would do anything rather than be forced to this pass. And their friends tried their best to see to it (by sending round the basin, giving them some of their own stock to sell, holding an auction or a concert) that they should be kept from this final ignominy. The trouble was that the bad times which affected one coster, affected all the other costers at the same time. For a coster it was far more honourable to assault a policeman and be sent to jail for so doing, than to go to the workhouse for aid. 'Him? Oh he's only been quodded for pitching into a crusher.' Moreover (though this did not enter into his consideration) he would be fed better in prison than his ordinary fare outside prison.

We have the careful records of prison doctors and dieticians on the minimum food they regarded as essential to maintain life in jail, con-sistent with keeping the cost at the lowest possible expenditure. They had worked out a diet of 168 ounces per week of solid food. Prisoners incurring hard labour needed a minimum of 254 ounces of solid food. Ordinary costers on their ordinary daily rounds worked as hard as hard labour prisoners, and longer hours, on a diet of only 122 ounces of solid food per week. So a coster sent to jail and sentenced to hard labour

*English costers declared the Irish undercut them, sold inferior food, and were intruders who had no feeling for England.

would in fact be twice as well off for food, apart from the glory.

It was not only despair at having failed that made the workhouse so humiliating for the costers. It was the contempt and parsimony with which they were treated when they did finally, all else having failed, bring themselves to apply for help. This treatment was deliberate. The local authorities wanted above all to keep down the rates. Therefore applicants for charity must be made to feel so degraded that they would do anything rather than apply. Dickens has immortalised this in his *Christmas Carol*.

The workhouse separated men from their wives – breaking lifetime unions in order to send them to separate establishments.

Mayhew instances a former docker who had broken his leg in the course of his work, been obliged to spend many months in different hospitals as it refused to heal and he dreaded having it amputated. A variety of attempts to scrape a living by huckstering having failed, and with the responsibility of six children, too young to earn, and a wife whose scrubbing and laundering brought in very little, he was finally obliged to swallow his pride and apply to the Parish for relief.

The Parish, after the closest enquiry, allowed him for a strictly limited period, two shillings and sixpence a week, plus four loaves, stamped with the Parish stamp. He would have been much better off in jail.

So deeply has Union charity scarred the race memory of poor Londoners that today (when the Welfare State allots special sums for the relief of the aged and needy, and takes pains to advertise these available benefits in the national press and in every Post Office) there are still old people needing help who would rather remain in want than apply for the help available, which they feel would undermine their self-respect to accept. Social workers, trained in tact and understanding, who call on them to explain that they have earned help by their lifetime of work and that the country *wants* them to have it, are greeted with stubborn refusal and angry resentment. Something of Dickens' hateful workhouse taint still lingers.

COSTERS' FUNERALS

As leaders of their own society, the costers did everything they could to keep other costers off the Parish. Above all they were determined that every coster should have a fine funeral and never suffer the final humiliation of being buried by the Parish.

An East End court and its communal water pump.
1892.

No-one knew better than poor Londoners what needed to be done to make their lives endurable. No-one knew better than the costers how to give so that the recipient should not be humiliated. In fact no-one understood better than they did both the need for charity and the right way to provide it. And this understanding became the powerhouse which launched the Pearlies.

However poor a coster might be, when he died he died in the knowledge that his coster mates would see him out in style. This was, and still is, the poor Londoner's declaration that the dead man had been somebody, a man not a cypher, and that his life of brutish hardship and privation should not pass away unhonoured. It was their way of pointing out that the dead man had tried his best and that he deserved public recognition and respect for his effort. It was also, in fine cockney style, cocking a snoot at the police who had harried him in life, and the Establishment who would have dishonoured him in death by a pauper's funeral.

To raise money for a good 'send-off', all available means were put into action. In the first place, the process was at work before he actually died. No coster was ever allowed to die alone. If in hospital, his mates would take turns to sit with him (and the dying coster well knew how costly in terms of livelihood were the hours thus spent). They would bring him little treats of tea and sugar and cheer him up with raucous stories.

Costers in Mayhew's time rarely lived into old age, their lives were too hard. They suffered from rheumatism and tuberculosis and were accident-prone by the nature of their work. Nearly always they left a widow with young children.

The costers raised money for a slap-up coster funeral in various ways. There were pub concerts, each coster doing a turn before the basin was passed round for the collection. The costers also held raffles which added the pleasure of a gamble to the good cause. A kingsman would be contributed by one coster for which 3d and 6d raffle tickets would be sold. The drawing of the lucky ticket was always the occasion for a eulogy of the dead coster.

Often the lucky winner of the kingsman would generously hand it back again for a further raffle. These raffles took place at the local beer-shop or gin-palace in a heady atmosphere of noise and mounting excitement. Costers prided themselves on the amount of money they could raise communally when they tried. But the most important part of the enterprise (the 'brick' or 'friendly lead') took place in the dead coster's home.

Every coster entering the shabby room would drop a coin on the plate, as large a coin as he could manage. If the deceased had made any enemies in life amongst his fellow costers it was a point of honour that these should attend his wake and drop in a larger contribution than the rest. Thus death dissolved all coster feuds save only the eternal coster feud against the police.

A chairman and vice-chairman presided. Pots of beer circulated. Everyone wore their best. The coster girls criticised each other's bonnets and the young coster bucks took an occasional good-natured bash at each other's smart caps. The wake was deliberately conducted

An East End street waits for a fever patient to be
taken off to the local hospital.

with jocularity. Mild horseplay was encouraged, for there must be no
melancholy to mar the occasion. This was in striking contrast to the
cultivated gloom of middle-class English funerals of the period.

By the Costers' credo their dead mate had lived hard, faced misfortune
without flinching and without complaint. He had done his best in life,
faced up gallantly to the police and stood by his pals. Now they were
gathered together to see that he went out not in sorrow but in style.

Hammering on the table, the chairman roared for silence. He then
called upon everyone present (man, woman and child) by name and in
turn, to oblige the company with a song, dance, anecdote, or musical
turn. Every coster could play something, fiddle, melodeon, tin whistle,
jews-harp, comb, spoons, make bird noises, or perform a clog dance.

43

Boy. "No' why don't you NEVER TREAT YOURSELF TO NO LUXURIES, GUVNER?"

Mostly the company obliged by a song. It was a point of etiquette that every song must be cheerful. No-one appreciated a doleful song more than the costers – a doleful song in its rightful place, and its rightful place was definitely not at a wake. 'The 'at my father wore', 'Any old iron', were considered suitable items. All costers were passionate afficionados of the penny gaffs and music halls, and knew all the popular songs by heart. And the beer circulated continually.

There was this strong feeling, which was to be the basis of the Pearly organisation of the future, that it is proper to offer entertainment when you are asking for donations. They were not paupers. They were not begging. They were offering something for something, and offering it in the recognised cockney way, heartily and with panache.

When the Chairman decided that the Concert had reached its climax and the plate at the door was comfortably loaded, they all adjourned to the local beer-house taking the dead coster's widow with them. When they finally took her home, with the consoling assurance that the funeral the next day was going to be spectacular, they left her with enough money to buy stock, pay her rent and feed the children for a time.

The rule was that the poorer the coster at the time of his death the more important and brilliant his funeral had to be. One coster who died young left less than two shillings in the world. Nevertheless owing to the efforts of his mates, headed by his pal George, no less than £5 worth of flowers adorned his coffin which on its way to the cemetery was preceded by a splendid band, hired at a cost of fifty shillings.

No coster went to his grave without the dignity of twenty or thirty vehicles following him (mainly donkeycarts). Even if a 'walking funeral' was the best that could be achieved an impressive cortège would follow his coffin, and each coster mourner would be marvellously dressed up in his best and adorned with bright flowers and a brilliant kingsman.

So the costers, who entered life crudely, were named without a christening, courted hastily, coupled without benefit of clergy and raised a family without education or hope of improvement, were buried magnificently, stopping the traffic in death which they had never been allowed to do in life.

But if death was something costers could look forward to, safe in the knowledge that their mates would see to it that they would be well done by, there was first life to be got through.

COSTER FAMILIES

Like their customers, costers lived close to the edge of want. Mayhew's careful calculations worked out their average profit per week as ten shillings. Some weeks were better but many were worse. Wet weather was always disastrous. The Royal Society calculated that in London rain falls an average of three days each week, nearly every other day throughout the year. No wonder the costers were fatalists.

The alleys and courts where the costers rented their rooms have still survived in many parts of South and East London, Soho and Holborn. Leather Lane, always an important coster market, still retains something of its former crowded jollity and irregular eating habits. The courts are without pavements. Formerly there was an old pump in the middle of each court (usually dangerously insanitary) which catered for the neighbourhood.

In such courts generations of costers were born, left as infants in the care of children (too young themselves to go selling in the streets) whilst coster mothers were out with their shallows. Mothers had their babies brought to them to be suckled on their rounds. At the age of five coster children knew how to buy, arrange and cry their small stock, and by the age of seven the little girls were already old hands at the business. Hawking was the only education their parents could give them, and they never dreamed of becoming anything else but costers.

Boys at this age would be taken on as 'cryers' by costers who had lost their own voices by over use, or sometimes went with their father to cry for him and learn the trade by observation. They were reputed to be extremely sharp. They worked for an occasional meal and 'bunts'* and a little pocketmoney. By the time they were fourteen boys were ready to start off on their own. And by the age of fifteen or sixteen they had usually got themselves a girl, left the parental room and set up for themselves. Costers did not 'marry' with a religious or even a civil ceremony. They just moved into a room together (rent about 4/6 a week). Such free marriages were neither more nor less faithful than legitimate ones, and the children born of such unions were acknowledged. 'Chance children' were brought up with the rest without rancour.

COSTER EDUCATION 1851

Even with every member of the family working hard and for long hours (father with pushcart, mother with shallow, the young daughters with shoulder or hip trays and the boys hired out to other costers) coster families would be pushed to make a living. From the tenderest age little coster girls were given a few pennies to invest for themselves in flowers or watercress, which they would refashion, sitting on the market steps, into small bunches to be cried all day. Sometimes they would be beaten if they did not sell out before they returned home in the evening. Their parents no doubt believed this was the best education for the hard life they were already bound to. There was no question of schooling or even learning to read and write. Costers could not see what use such time-consuming accomplishments could be to costers.

'The Select Committee on Education of the Poorer Classes' (1837–1838) reported that only one out of twelve children of poor families received any kind of education: only one in twenty-four any kind of education of any use to them. (It was worse further North in the large industrial cities. Birmingham educated one child only out of twenty-four, Manchester one out of thirty-eight and Leeds only one out of every

*Any extra money earned by sales in addition to the expected earnings. Frequently spelt 'bunce' today.

forty-one. In all over two million children of working-class English parents received no education at all.)

The reason was these children were much more useful to employers as cheap labour in the factories and mines, and their parents' wages were so low that, like the London costers, they could not survive without their children's small earnings to augment the family income.* When trade declined it was these unemployed families who trekked on foot to London to swell the ranks of street hucksters.

By 1875 elementary education had been established in England, but this was not made compulsory for another twenty years. Even then attendance was irregular or non-existent because in poor families the

---

*An Act was in operation by the 1900s whereby the brightest children were encouraged to leave school at 13, instead of the regulation 14 years of age, rather than try for higher education.

children's earnings were needed at home. They had to stay at home to mind the babies, or else bring the baby to school with them whilst the mother went out to work. School teachers reported later that when the children did come to school (and classes were never less than fifty or sixty pupils) they were already so exhausted from having worked since daybreak without food that they were unable to learn. It was found that before these children could take in what was being taught they needed food, and if they were to come to school in bad weather they needed shoes.

Apprenticeships cost money. Few parents could afford them. Even going into domestic service needed an outlay for uniforms, well beyond the means of poor parents. A lad hoping to enter the mercantile marine the hard way had to bring with him his own bed linen and uniforms. There seemed no way out of the vicious circle of poverty and ignorance proliferating more ignorance and more poverty.

But the half-starved and uneducated cockneys and their children had one unfailing outlet. They were all born entertainers. And foremost among them were the costers.

EAST LONDON ENTERTAINMENT

East End children could turn their hands to anything and learned early to chat up potential customers. Boys sold 'lights' (matches) at street corners, hung about cabstands ready to hold the horse's reins, swept street-crossings, and entertained passers-by with feats of tumbling, songs and tricks. Little girls were always ready to dress up and sing or do a turn and take a collection. Nathaniel Hawthorne reported in 1855:

Tumblers, hand-organists, puppet-showmen, musicians, Highland bag-pipers, and all such vagrant mirthmakers, are very numerous in the streets of London. A multitude of Punches go the rounds continually.

The most obvious feature of London slum life, which Dickens described, Mayhew noted, Phil May drew, but Jack London missed, was the amount and rich variety of entertainment the local people enjoyed on their very doorstep. Apart from the impromptu nightly concerts in every public house, which presently developed into the famous music halls, and the bawdy 'penny gaffs' which so horrified Mayhew, every street seemed to have some kind of entertainment going on all day.

Wandering groups of musicians, solitary singers, barrel-organs (with a live monkey dressed like a Neapolitan), – free music to which the

The costers through foreign eyes: another drawing
by G. Scharf depicts a Covent Garden stall and its
proprietor in 1818.

children danced in the streets – sometimes a one-man band, or a real
German band. There were paper-tearers, Punch & Judy and shadow
shows. Even the act of buying a halfpennyworth of parsnips from an
itinerant coster's barrow became, by virtue of mutual backchat, as good
as a music-hall turn.

Theatre in all its forms has always been the lifeblood of Londoners.
Those costers who could afford the threepenny gallery of the Coburg
Theatre, known as the 'Vic', were given better entertainment than the
penny gaffs. The gallery could hold up to 2000 people and it was always
packed to suffocation.

The audience knew exactly what they wanted, whistling shrilly at a
well-executed hornpipe, booing at sentimental passages they felt to be

false, encouraging the heroine to chastise Russian soldiers (at the time of the Crimean War), – shouting 'Go it my tulip', and demanding of the orchestra (who could not be heard for the noise from the gallery): 'Now then you catgut scrapers! Let's have a ha'purth of liveliness!'

The sceneshifter was exhorted to 'Higher the blue' or 'Light up the moon' if the gallery couldn't see what they had paid for. The costers liked dances and comic songs better than anything else. And they loved to join in the choruses. Singers always allowed for audience participation and the programme was printed with the words 'assisted by the most numerous and effective chorus in the metropolis', meaning the costers in the gallery.

The most popular song by far was 'Ducklegged Dick', which was, noted Mayhew, 'invariably insisted on whether in keeping with the drama or planned in the official programme or not'. 'Ducklegged Dick' is a coster song about costers, their donkeys and their unending feud with the police. It is fortunate that Mayhew has left us the words, for, so far, I have been unable to trace the music. It can be called a ballad and it sets down firmly the coster philosophy of Fatalism, Luck, Chance:

> Ducklegged Dick had a donkey
> And his lush* loved much for to swill
> One day he got rather lumpy
> And got sent seven days to the mill†
> His donkey was taken to the greenyard‡
> A fate which he never deserved
> Oh it was such a regular mean yard
> That alas the poor moke got starved.

CHORUS:
> *Oh bad luck can't be prevented*
> *Fortune she smiles or she frowns*
> *He's best off that's contented*
> *To mix, Sirs, the ups and the downs.*

COSTERS & SATURDAY NIGHT MARKETS

No less exciting than the penny gaffs and the Coburg were the Saturday night street markets where in a pandemonium of noise the costers counted on selling enough stock to make up their week's earnings.

*Woman, sweetheart. †Treadmill. ‡Prison.

Everyone turned up to stare, haggle, enjoy the street shows, exchange gossip, have a row, treat themselves to small luxuries and buy their precious Sunday dinner. The crowd had been paid for their week's labour and were eager to spend their earnings.

The markets were lit by acetylene lamps, naphtha flares, ship's lanterns, candles stuck into turnips. Everyone, including the costers themselves, enjoyed the scene. Baked chestnuts, blacking, Yarmouth bloaters, fourpenny bonnets (sold from an upturned umbrella), whelks, walnuts – all were cried in shrill voices. Begging rhymes, bamboo flute-playing, peepshows, shadow-shows, acrobats, three-card tricks, song sellers, enlivened the market.

Through this crowd the costers pushed and bellowed: 'Ho-ho! Hi-i-i-i! What do you think of this 'ere! A penny a bunch! Hurrah for free trade! 'Ere's your turnips!', and coster boys setting out for themselves cried, 'A double 'andful of fine parsley for a penny!' All struggling, as Mayhew comments, 'to get the penny profit out of the poor man's Sunday dinner'. It was (and still is) in these markets that the Pearlies in due course took their place.

COSTERS & SUNDAY MORNING MARKETS

There were also the Sunday morning markets, geared to those who had missed the Saturday night market either because the temptation of the pub had been too great or they had got there so late that there was little left to buy. There was a chastened air about these Sunday morning markets. The neighbouring shops would all be closed and shuttered. The housewives hastily choosing turnips or cabbages (which they stowed in their white aprons), their menfolk lounging about with their pet terriers under their arms, or hands in pockets.

At 11 o'clock sharp the clocks struck and the policeman, in clean white gloves, forcibly closed the market, driving the street sellers out. It was now the Sabbath, and though none of them went to church, the church was there to go to.

Costers hated the Sunday morning markets, and if trade has been so bad that they were obliged to attend, felt embarrassed and ashamed. Sunday was their traditional day off. On Sundays they togged themselves up (they usually could afford to sport a fine silk 'kingsman' and if they had no family responsibilities they might even have a best suit) and took their girls out on the river or up to Hampstead Heath.

COSTERS & THE LAW

The delicate economic balance between costers and their customers could be destroyed overnight. The cholera epidemics of 1831 and 1849 brought ruin to thousands of London costers. A spell of cold, wet weather was fatal. These could be considered as acts of God. It was an Act of Parliament which brought so many London costers to the workhouse.

The London shopkeepers, who advertised their wares not by shouting but on printed bills, and who paid rates on their shops, hated the costers. Shopkeepers could get costers arrested by complaining that they were loitering, upon which complaint the police could arrest the costers and seize their handcarts and stock. This inflammable situation came to a head when Parliament passed the Michael Angelo Taylor Act, known as the Police Act (1850) – which ordered the instant removal of any street traders on representation by the local shopkeepers that the street traders were injuring their trade.

The first removals, on such local representations, took place in the flourishing coster market in Leather Lane, Holborn, and resulted not only in ruining the costers but also in ruining the shopkeepers as well, for no customer came near Leather Lane at all. The place was deserted. All the customers took their custom to other street markets elsewhere. After a grim fortnight with no trade the shopkeepers of Leather Lane gave in and asked the police authorities to reverse their previous decision.

But in Lambeth market, on representation, not from the Lambeth shopkeepers but the parishioners of nearby Christ Church, Blackfriars Road, that the Lambeth costers were injuring their trade, these costers were driven from their stands and ruined. From scraping a bare living they now had no living at all. Coster families broke up as each member wandered elsewhere to try some other trade. There was unusual resentment from other costers as they encroached upon their rounds. Many ruined costers had to face the ultimate degradation and apply to the 'Big House'.

'Perhaps they'll give me nothing', one coster told Mayhew, 'but take me in, and that's hard on a man as don't want to be a pauper'.

Some workhouses which did not wish to incur the expense of taking a coster and his family into their care made a practice of starting him in business again by a donation of five or even ten shillings. But as soon as he set up the Police Act would be invoked as before and the same procedure reduce him to ruin.

Coster girls, Mayhew noted, so feared the Big House that they now preferred to take to prostitution to earn their living, or even break a window and get taken off to jail.

There also began the practice of bribery. Shopkeepers who had denounced the costers and had them removed by the police presently allowed them to return on payment of a sweetener, such as six shillings a week (even as much as eight shillings), for permission to trade. In such a fraught situation the opportunities for bribery and tale-bearing were rife. Everyone concerned came out worse, because the money the 'Big House' used to relieve the distressed costers was raised by increasing local rates which the incensed shopkeepers, who had driven the costers into pauperism, were themselves obliged to pay.

COSTERS & THE POLICE

There were uprisings and revolutions throughout Europe in the 19th century and the British Government, fearing to appear weak, exerted harsh control over the poor. Mayhew, as we have said, estimated that in 1850 there were between 30,000 and 40,000 costers on the streets of London – a formidable force and all police-haters.

'The hatred of the costermonger to a Peeler was intense, and with their opinion of the police, all the more ignorant unite that of the governing power. I am assured that in case of a political riot every coster would seize his policeman.' The same story was told to Mayhew by different costers: 'Can you wonder at it, sir, that I hate the police? They drive us about. We must move on, we can't stand here and we can't pitch there. But if we're "cracked up", that is if we're forced to go to the Union (I've known it both at Clerkenwell and the City of London Workhouses), why the Parish gives us money to buy a barrow or a shallow, or to hire them and leave the 'house and start for ourselves: and what's the use of that if the police won't let us sell our goods? Which is right – The Parish or the police?'

The police wore heavy protective clothing, could quickly call reinforcements, and carried heavy batons. The penalties for assaulting the police were extremely severe, and a criminal offence could be and often was punished by transportation or by the treadmill.

The costers always closed ranks against the police, working out ingenious ways of irritating them. Young boys, for instance, would jibe at policemen, keeping just out of reach of their flailing batons. One very common procedure, Mayhew reports, when a policeman was trying to arrest a coster for standing still, was as follows:

If a policeman has seized a barrow, it is customary to whip off the wheels while the officers have gone for assistance – for a large and loaded barrow requires two men to convey it to the greenyard. This is done with great dexterity: and the next step is to dispose of the stock to any passing costers or to any 'standing' in the neighbourhood, and it is honestly accounted for. The policemen on their return find an empty and unwheelable barrow, which they must carry off by main strength, amid the cheers of the populace.

The coster could depend on getting back his stock, or its financial equivalent, when he came out of jail a hero.

COSTERS' SLANG

The coster's slang (of which fragments are still current today) concerned itself with money, beer, police, women, bargains, marketing, approval and disapproval. It was accompanied by nods, winks, shrugs, emphasis of tone and inflection, and could be embellished with extra syllables or fancy endings at will.

A 'flatch' meant a halfpenny. A 'yenep', a penny. 'Owt-yenep', twopence. 'Erth-yenep', threepence. 'Rouf-yenep', fourpence. And so on to 'leven', eleven pence, and 'gen', twelve pence. 'Yenep-flatch' was three halfpence. A sovereign was called a 'couter', a half sovereign a 'half couter' or 'net gen'. Fifteen shillings was 'erth-ewif-gens'.

A coster told Mayhew, 'The Irish can't tumble to it anyway. The Jews can tumble better,* but we're their masters. Some of the young salesmen at Billingsgate understand us, but *only* at Billingsgate; and they think they're uncommon clever but they're not up to the mark. The police don't understand us at all. *It would be a pity if they did.*'

'Cool the esclop' meant 'Look at the police'. 'Cool the namesclop' meant 'Look at the policeman'. 'Cool ta the dilo nemo' meant 'Look at the old woman'. This was a derisive remark, applied to any woman of any age who appeared to be giving herself airs. 'A doogheno or dabheno' meant a 'bad market'. 'On' meant 'no'. 'Say' meant 'yes'. 'Tumble to your barrikin' meant 'Understand you'. 'Top o' reeb' meant 'pot of

*The name 'Fagin' in Charles Dickens's Oliver Twist is the Yiddish word for thief, 'ganef', in backwards slang.

beer'. 'Doing rab' meant 'doing badly'. 'Kennetseeno' meant 'stinking' (fish). 'Flatch kanurd' meant 'Half drunk'. 'Flash it' meant 'show it' (still in use today). 'On doog', 'no good'. 'Cross chap' meant 'a thief'. 'Showfulls' meant 'bad money'. 'Im on to the deb' meant 'I am going to bed'. 'To the tightne', 'to dinner'. 'Nommus' meant 'be off', and 'Tol', 'a lot' or share or stock.

Any coster was welcome to add to this stock of slang calculated to mystify and irritate the police. Backwards slang was succeeded by rhyming slang.

COSTERS' DONKEYS

In Mayhew's time costers usually bought their donkeys at Smithfield Market on a Friday. A major purchase as vital and substantial an investment for them as buying a house is today to a young couple on small means. There was a fair held between one and five o'clock for the convenience of the costers where up to 200 donkeys would be offered for sale. Many young coster lads hung about trying to make themselves useful and, eager to be associated with this particular world, would race the donkeys and display their fine points whilst disparaging donkeys in the care of other lads.

Foodstalls offered whelks at these Donkey Fairs for a halfpenny, new milk, 'ha'penny a mugfull. New milk from the keow!', and pea soup by the cupful besides hot eels, slices of cake, apples, nuts, and pineapple rock.

Since much bitterness was later caused by social workers complaining that costers were cruel to their donkeys, it is as well to set down here what Mayhew said in 1851.

The costermongers almost universally treat their donkeys with kindness. Many a costermonger will resent the ill-treatment of a donkey as he would a personal indignity. These animals are often not only favourites but pets, having their share of the costermonger's dinner when bread forms a portion of it, or pudding, or anything suited to the palate of the brute. Those well-used manifest fondness for their masters and are easily manageable . . .

Apart from their natural affection for animals, these donkeys were the costers' living and good feeding was vital to their welfare.

The usual fare of a donkey is a peck of chaff which costs one penny a quart of oats and a quart of beans each averaging three halfpence, being an expendi-

MALAPROPOS

Mrs Snobson (*who is doing a little slumming for the first time and wishes to appear affable, but is at a loss to know how to commence conversation*): "TOWN VERY EMPTY!"

A sketch by Phil May dating from 1899 which captures the unease of the charity ladies from the West End when confronted with the reality of the East End.

ture of fourpence or fivepence a day; but some give double this quantity in a prosperous time. Only one meal a day is given. Their donkeys lived well when they themselves lived well.

If the average earning of a coster amounted to no more than 10/- weekly, the 2/4 or 2/11 for the donkey's food amounted to a considerable outlay. The following story of a coster's donkey was related to Mayhew.

'There was a friend of mine who had great trouble about his donkey a few months back. I saw part of it and knew all about it. He was doing a little work at Wandsworth on a Sunday morning and the poor thing fell down dead. He was very fond of his donkey and kind to it, and the donkey was very fond of him. He thought he wouldn't leave the poor creature he'd had a good while, and had been out with in all weathers, by the roadside: so he dropped all notion of doing business, and with help got the poor dead thing into his cart – its head lollopping over the end of the cart and its poor eyes staring at nothing. He thought he'd drag it home and bury it somewhere. It wasn't for the value he dragged it home — for what's a donkey worth? There was a few persons about and they was all quiet and seemed sorry for the poor fellow and his donkey; but the church bells struck up, and up came a "crusher" and took the man up and next day he was fined 10/-. I can't exactly say for what. He never saw no more of the animal and lost his stock as well as his donkey.'

A typical ending, the costers declared, to any encounter with the police.

COSTERS & DO-GOODERS

The police protected the wealthy and the upper-class, complained the costers, including those unwelcome 'do-gooders' who came snooping round the costers' courts and alleys, asking prying questions, ordering them about, lecturing them on how to bring up their children, denouncing their amusements and handing out tracts.

Since 'do-gooding' was becoming fashionable in London society (and therefore attracting the socially ambitious wives and daughters of wealthy merchants, whose taint of trade would otherwise prevent them from achieving social contact with high society), the costers had become a target for these hated visits.

The failure of many of the do-gooders to understand the conditions they were inspecting was profound. One such lady, who had managed to get into a coster's home in his absence, earnestly advised the coster's common-law wife to buy a separate bed for each of her numerous children and to teach them modesty by bathing each one in private. A child's bed, she assured her, could be bought for a mere eighteen shillings. Like other coster families this one lived all in one room, without running water, and their total weekly income amounted to considerably less than eighteen shillings.

There were of course honourable exceptions – do-gooders who really did good. Outstanding amongst those were Baroness Burdett-Coutts and Mrs Catherine Gladstone (wife of William Ewart Gladstone). Baroness Burdett-Coutts was a friend of Charles Dickens whose advice she sought in her charitable work. The coster girls presented her with a silver statuette of a coster flower girl in gratitude for her work for them. Catherine Gladstone won the respect of the East End when she insisted on attending the London Hospital daily during the cholera epidemic of 1864. These two ladies are still remembered in East London as 'true friends of the poor'.

But there were far more lady do-gooders whom the costers regarded as snoopers and tried to keep out. These lady missionaries, balked because their efforts to evangelise the ungodly costers had proved fruitless, altered their tactics and presently launched new campaigns, directed against their women and their donkeys.

Coster girls in the third quarter of the 19th century were renowned for their repartee and their dashing dress. Lady dress-reformers now started a campaign to force them to wear 'modest dress'. This reformed dress included a drab-coloured shapeless overall, and a small close-fitting bonnet (unbecoming versions of an outmoded earlier fashion). No waistline, no feathers, no buttons.

Only one coster girl (temporarily in their control as a skivvy) was known to put on this reformed dress. Her coster friends, on her day off, jeered it off the London streets for good.

The donkey campaign was more successful. The coster who had succeeded in acquiring a donkey and therefore joined the coster élite, would build a stable for it out of old fruit crates in his backyard. The lady social reformers launched a violent campaign against these home-made stables, 'cruel, heartless, unhygienic'.

They organised the building of airy commodious donkey stables which they forced the costers to rent 'at viable rents' – viable that is for the landlords. This extra strain on their slender and fluctuating earnings was more than the costers could tolerate. They bitterly resented the imputation that they did not look after their donkeys properly and contrasted the missionary ladies' concern for their donkeys' lodging with their total disregard for the abysmal lodging of the costers themselves.

So the costers had two rentals to pay and became dependent on the approved new donkey-stables, a situation which was to have a disastrous consequence a century later.

Baroness Burdett-Coutts encouraged the costers in competitions they understood and enjoyed – donkey and pony races and parades at Epsom and the Derby and Kensington Palace Fields – competitions, which were very popular, for the best turn-out with the award of silver cups for the winners. These competitions have survived into our own times.

COSTER DRESS .

Nineteenth century English working people dressed according to their work, so that it was possible to tell at a glance what was a man's job. The exception to this were the very poorest who wore third- and fourth-hand clothes, often of superior origin but in the last stages of decay. Dickens complained that London dockers (then the poorest of the poor) went about their work grotesquely tricked up in decrepit tail-coats and bashed-in old top hats.

The costers, highest in the ranks of street traders, had evolved a distinctive dress of their own and were proud of it. As early as 1834 Dickens mentions a costermongers' outfitters, in the Ratcliffe Highway, where already pearl buttons (to become such a rage 50 years later) glittered on coster waistcoats. The London costers were a close community which held together firmly and developed its own distinct identity, marked out by its own special dress. Costers took up with other costers and brought up their children to be costers. They spent time, thought and more than they could afford to dress well in their own image.

The dress of coster girls moved with the basic fashion of the day and always included an apron. In Mayhew's time coster girls wore printed cotton, a dark tight-fitting bodice, full skirts over which was tied a clean white apron, a dark shawl and a small round bonnet set over a net cap. As coster girls carried heavy baskets on their heads their bonnets were usually crushed and flattened. They wore shorter skirts and petti-coats than other girls, showing their ankles and boots. Little coster girls

went barefoot and wore second-hand clothes until they were earning.

Coster youths, free from many of the responsibilities of older costers, and eager to cut a dash, were especially dressy. In the 1850s they wore their hair long in front, twisted into figure-6 curls, or twisted back to their ears in the 'Newgate-knocker' style. It was a particular source of anger against the Police that when in 'Quod all along of muzzling the bobbies' their carefully cultivated long hair was cropped short.

Coster youths wore a small worsted or plush flapped tie-up cap, possibly introduced into London at that time by Polish and Russian emigrés. These strong caps had a practical purpose because baskets were carried on the head. Coats were rarely worn, lest they impede free movement. Waistcoats were a vital assertion of coster personality.

These waistcoats were strongly made of corduroy, broadribbed and long, worn buttoned up close to the throat and with fustian sleeves. The waistcoat sported two, often four, large flapped pockets. If the corduroy waistcoat was light in colour (sand-colour was considered very smart), then the waistcoat buttons were made of brass with a 'sporting' design in relief of a fox's or stag's head. Alternatively, light-coloured waistcoats sported black bone buttons with a design of bright flowers. On dark corduroy waistcoats, smoked mother-of-pearl buttons were particularly favoured. Here we have a firm foundation for what half a century later was to develop into the extraordinary cult of the 'Pearlies'.

Coster trousers were usually made of cable-cord, dark (ratskin) in colour, fitting tightly to the knee and cut wide at the ankles where they almost, but not quite, covered the boots. They were cut on the same lines as sailors' trousers. Those costers who dealt in fish wore in addition a large apron of blue serge which could be tucked up round the waist.

Mayhew records that the coster's chief pride was his boots and his kingsman. Yellow flowers on a green ground or red and blue strong patterns were greatly admired. To be without a splendid silk kingsman was the stigma of failure. Costers liked to wear their kingsman loosely wrapped round their throats with the ends dangling over their waistcoats.

Fifty years later, Gus Elen, the famous singer of coster songs (who used so traditional a cockney idiom that Sam Weller himself would have been at home with it) modelled his stage costume on real coster dress

A London hot potato-vendor – such street traders were a common sight in the 1890s.

chosen from the lower ranks of costers. The dress included a horizontally striped jersey, a vivid kingsman, dark checked jacket, trousers bordered with pearl buttons, and a black bowler hat encircled with a wreath of bright flowers like a Morris dancer.

Girl costers also wore a kingsman, tied at the neck with the ends tucked neatly into their bodices. Costers loved to own a variety of kingsmen and could rarely resist the temptation to add to them when they were in funds. An enamoured coster would declare his passion by the gift of a kingsman to his sweetheart. It was a black day when he had to pawn his kingsman.

The coster's boots were as vital to his profession as to his self-respect. A coster could always be identified by his boots. No matter how desperate his economic situation his boots were always the very last things to be pawned. For a coster to be forced to buy and wear second-hand boots was considered a bitter degradation. Strong boots were vital because, as we have noted, costers trudged at least ten miles a day pushing a heavy barrow over the London cobblestones. The costers' pride took the form of fancy uppers ornamented with such British emblems as a heart or thistle surrounded by a wreath of roses.

Coster girls, too, needed strong boots.

According to Mayhew coster girls wore printed-cotton summer and winter. Coster women wore a shawl if they could afford one when the weather was bitter. Wool was too expensive to be considered, and silk despised by coster girls (except for kerchiefs) as the mark of the rich parasite, only suitable for whores. Their practical and coquettish short skirts revealed their boots and they wore white stockings. They carried their shallows or 'prickles' (special baskets for carrying walnuts) on their heads, suspended from their shoulders, or if exceptionally heavy, tied firmly round their waists.

Costers were very particular about the dress and behaviour of their women-folk. They expected their girls to be clean, neatly dressed, lively but demure when they took them out to the theatre or to a 'twopenny hop'. They were not permitted to 'show their necks', that is wear low-cut bodices, in coster understanding the mark of ladies in society or whores.

In the 1850s there were, according to Mayhew, only five tailors in all London who knew how to make proper coster dress. Costers, so exploited themselves, were eager to stamp out sweated labour in the making of their clothes and boycotted those tailors known to underpay their workgirls.

Here is the advertisement of a costers' outfitters, 1850. It is artfully written in the vernacular, though not one in ten costers could read.

ONCE TRY
YOU'LL COME AGAIN!

Slap-up tog and out-and-out KICKSIES builder. *Mr. Field* nabs the chance of putting his customers *awake,* that he has just made his escape from *Russia,* not forgetting to clap upon some of the right sort of BUCKS, to make single and double backed slops for gentlemen in black, when on his return home he was stunned to find one of the top manufacturers of *Manchester* had cut his lucky and stepped off to the *Swan Stream,* leaving behind him a valuable stock of –

Moleskins, Cords, Velveteens, Plushes, Swansdowns, etc.

and I having some ready in my kick, grabbed the chance and stepped home with my swag, and am now safe landed at my crib. I can turn out toggery of every description, *very* slap up, at the following low prices for –

READY GILT! (Tick being no go)

Upper Benjamin, built on a downey plan, a monarch to half a finnuff; Slap-up *Velveteen Togs,* lined with the same, 1 pound 1 quarter and a peg. *Moleskin ditto,* any colour, lined with the same – 1 couter. One pair of *Kerseymere Kicksies,* any colour, built very slap-up with the artful dodge, a canary. *Pair of stout cord ditto,* made very saucy, nine bob and a kick. *Pair of long sleeve moleskin,* all colours. built hanky-panky, with a double fakement down the side, and artful buttons at bottom, half a monarch. *Pair of stout ditto,* built very serious, nine times. *Pair of out-and-out fancy sleeve Kicksies,* cut to drop down on the Trotters, two bulls. *Waist Togs* cut long with Moleskin back and sleeve, ten pegs. *Blue cloth ditto,* cut slap, with pearl buttons, fourteen peg. *Mud pipes, Knee caps,* and *Trotter* cases built very low. *A decent allowance* made to SEEDY SWELLS, TEA KETTLE PURGERS, HEAD ROBBERS, and FLUNKEYS out of collar.

N.B. Gentlemen finding their own Broady can be accommodated.

EAST END LONDON IN 1900

In the fifty years between Mayhew's *Survey of the London Poor* and George R. Sims' *Living in London,* the population of Britain had enormously increased, by far the greater increase being below the poverty level.

HE: "Ere y'are lady; nice 'addick".

She "No, I don't like the look of that".

HE: "Well, if it's looks yer after, you want
a bloomin' gold-fish".

The coster's repartee: a charcoal drawing executed
by George Belcher for *The Tatler* magazine in 1926.

Sims wrote of the 'depths below depths' of poverty in London. The patrons of the Homes of the Shaftesbury Institute (which provided bed and breakfast of a sort for 2d) were dustbin-raiders, sellers of matches and bootlaces at street-corners, people who counted themselves lucky to earn sixpence a day. There were boy mudlarks squelching in the tidal Thames, children who tried to make a living by skimming off the débris from the Thames after a fire had damaged the warehouses on the wharves, children who ran after coal-carts to gather fragments to resell. East End girls worked sixteen hours a day on fine lingerie needle-work in West End factories for 4/6 a week. Shop assistants in the West End worked a 90-hour week, especially late on Saturday nights. All the well-known London restaurants cashed in on the sale of 'broken meats' (scraped off their customers' plates) to famished people waiting outside the back entrances.

The tunes of the Salvation Army may have been cheerful but their famous Shelters were gloomy. In 1892 in the Whitechapel Shelter the poor were permitted to sit till bedtime, but though a penny supper was available to those who could afford it, the rows of bunks were packed tightly end to end and looked like coffins, and a large notice on the wall demanded ARE YOU READY TO DIE? Prayers were compulsory. There was another kind of 'Penny sit-up' Shelter for those still poorer, where clients were allowed to sit all night leaning forward against a rope.

A disproportionate number of the third of English people who lived below the poverty line lived in London. A pointer to the general state of debility is the fact that more than one-third of the recruits for service in the Boer War had to be rejected on medical grounds, being below the necessary minimum standard of health regarded as essential.

DOMESTIC SERVICE

Advertisement of the time:

HOUSEMAIDS!
Wages £18 a year
NO BEER NO FRINGES

PARLOURMAIDS!
Wages £22 a year
NO BEER NO FRINGES

BETWEEN-MAID!
Wages £12.2.6d a year
NO BEER NO FRINGES

Aged 19. One in family.
Three other servants
kept.

Domestic service was hard to come by because strict references were essential. A flourishing trade in faked references supplied a living to astute scriveners. Domestic service (which needed, besides references, outlay for uniforms) was regarded as a profession out of reach of most poor girls. Nevertheless up to 1914 there were at least a million domestic servants working in London alone. They were considered lucky, being assured of bed and board at a period when so many of the poor had neither.

Jack London described the crammed workhouses with many applicants being turned away, and the hungry mobs swarming round the Salvation Army Shelters. In the summer of 1902 he tramped London with the down-and-outs. The law, he discovered, allowed the homeless to sit on steps or ground or bench, but not to go to sleep. Amongst these night wanderers were unemployed sailors. He calculated that one in every four adult Londoners by now died in the poorhouse, the asylum, or the infirmary.

Eighty thousand East Londoners went hop-picking in Kent each year. Though the pay was only one penny an hour, it was regarded as a holiday.

Jack London noted down sentences given by the courts. Seven days for a boy caught stealing fifteen peas from a lorry. Seven days for a fifteen-year old boy found sleeping on waste ground with no means of subsistence; one month for a man who had stolen nine ferns from a garden.

He recorded twenty people plus many children sharing six rooms and a large family renting one room and subletting part of that one room so that their three shillings rental would be reduced by the lodger paying one and six for his share of the room. 'No bathroom', he reported 'in the whole neighbourhood'.

He noted some of the wages, for example 30/- a week's pay for shoe-making, a fourteen hour day, and the shoemaker providing his own tools and cardboard.

One family he described, husband a gas-fitter (a T.U. member as it happened—for by then trades unions were legal), unskilled and not strong in health, helped by the earnings of his wife who worked from 4.30 a.m. till daylight faded making cloth dress-skirts (lined, with two flounces) for 7/- a dozen. Their daughter apprenticed to a dressmaker earned 1/6 a week, a trade from which she was sacked during the slack season. Their other daughter worked in a bicycle store for 5/- a week, walking two miles to work each day and two miles back. If late she was fined.

Jack London calculated that by the third generation strong country stock moving into London had already become degenerate and flaked out (a 5 foot 2 inch man weighing 10 stones, he recorded, considered himself very strong and hearty).

To pass as one of the London poor in order to find out what he wished to know (a gesture that probably deceived no-one but Jack London himself), he bought some slop-shop garments. Stout cord trousers, a frayed jacket, a thin leather belt, stiff heavy boots and a cap. The whole cost him 10/-.

Jack London's picture of the gloomy depths of East London poverty was carefully reported. All he noted was perfectly true. But yet it was not the whole story. What Jack London missed was the underlying cockney toughness, the resilience and the panache. Those East Enders he questioned drank with him, sometimes (as he appeared to them educated and better nourished than themselves) touched their caps and called him 'Sir' or 'Guvnor' which horrified him, but they certainly did not tell him everything. He did not, like so many reporters, go to the slums to pursue his enquiries accompanied by a plain-clothes police officer. He was, however, a stranger. He was a foreigner. Why didn't he mind his own business?

What Jack London missed were the cockney entertainments. He recorded the boozing but not the amusements. The East End music halls were then at their peak. Every pub had its nightly sing-songs. The trades union movement (which should have been of particular interest to him) was staging street demonstrations lit up by enormous brilliantly-hued political banners of gilded silk and brocade. And the Pearlies were already in action in their dazzling costumes.

What is most important about the London poor is their toughness and their humour. What matters most to them is their ability to organise themselves for what they want, in their own way. What is most significant to them is their innate patriotism, which has nothing to do with flag-wagging but springs from an unshakeable belief in themselves. I use the present tense because the East Enders have not changed in this respect.

These essential cockney qualities are rarely understood either by middle-class English observers or sensation-seeking foreign observers who realise that if they themselves were obliged to live in such slum conditions they could not survive. They would either emigrate or commit suicide. The 19th century London cockney did neither. He made up a song and dance about his misery and went to the music-hall for a good belly-laugh. He was adept at snatching wit from want.

'Night loafers' dossing down in the street and in doorways in the 1900s, waiting for parks to open, liked to congregate in Trafalgar Square conveniently near the parks and with useful fountains where they enjoyed a free wash and brush-up. It was the job of the police to wake them up all through the night and keep them moving. The night loafers, men women and children, despised the police and were not in the least intimidated by them. On the contrary, they felt the police should be grateful to them for providing the police with a job. They would retort – 'Where'd the likes of you be if it wasn't for the likes of us!'

COSTERS IN 1900

In 1900 George R. Sims reported that there were at least 60,000 costers trying to scrape a living in London. They tramped their beats for sixteen hours a day pushing barrows loaded with twelve cwt. of stock.

The typical coster lived in one room with his family, sleeping with his wife and youngest child on the only bed, the rest of the children sleeping on the floor among baskets and left-over vegetables.

Rheumatism, as well as tuberculosis, had become a major coster disability, for costers now had to go out on the streets wet or fine, not daring to miss a day. (Though those with donkeys would not venture to subject them to severe weather.) The wet coat spread on an old orange crate, to dry before the fire, was the symbol of the coster of 1900. Competition was fiercer than it had been fifty years before. Customers were poorer. The East End districts of London were now filled with political and religious refugees from Eastern Europe who lived on bread and tea and had no tradition of a Sunday dinner. In 1900 costers earned between 10/- and 12/- a week and 55% of their children died before the age of five.

The police continued to harrass costers. The instant a coster stopped on his rounds he could be arrested as before, for loitering, and dispossessed of his barrow and his stock. He now, however, had The Costermongers' Federation to which he subscribed. This was not a trade union, but an organisation which tried to fight for the rights of costers in the law courts, an expensive and fruitless battle.

The coster had no better opinion of the Establishment or the Church of England than his forebears. He now however, occasionally went through the ceremony of marriage, though without much conviction.

'When I got married', a coster told Sims, 'I come out of church and give my old woman two shillings and went back to work and didn't see her till 12.30 at night and hadn't a pound in the world'.

To encourage costers to submit to the church ceremony, churches offered 'multiple marriages' (ten couples at a time) usually on a Bank Holiday or Christmas, at a cheap all-in rate. There was also a well-known if dubious church in the East End which married youngsters for sevenpence and no questions asked, provided both partners were over fourteen years old.

The music halls produced a song to record this change to respectability. Wee Georgie Wood (the great star of the music halls, now well into his eighties) heard it in the 1890s as a child of eight. It was called 'The Coster's Wedding' and points out that it was the girl who was eager for a marriage ceremony not the coster:

> Today's the day
> The wedding bells will ring
> Today's the day
> I'll do the proper thing
> Though your name's Brown now
> Just hold your row
> You're going to change it soon.
> The parson's here
> What's going to marry us.
> A donkey cart
> Is going to carry us.
> And when the knot is tied
> And you're the blushing bride
> We're going upon our honeymoon.

I have recorded him singing it in the cockney accent of his youth, the words jolting out like lazy smallshot, the *a*'s all *i*'s – no *g*-endings, and the South London use of *f* for *th*.

The fashionable clergy and their mission-minded society ladies had kept up their tract-giving and poor visiting. 'Slumming' was more popular than ever, and the new trades unions were balefully regarded by them as a set-back to their mission, and a threat to their own economy.

'It won't do to make them too independent', one society lady warned.

'They go and join trades unions and a friend of mine lost quite a lot of money because his workmen joined a trades union.'

Society clergy had no doubts, however, that poverty had its purpose in the divine plan. 'In the absence of poverty' one fashionable priest assured his Mayfair congregation, 'the rich would have no-one upon whom to exercise their faculty for benevolence'.

EAST LONDON WEEK-END

Like Asian peasants, the London poor were always hopelessly in debt. Wages were very low, and there were so many fines at work to diminish even this low wage. Rents were so high in proportion to their earnings, and unemployment so frequent, that even those workers who drank but little and who were not burdened with many children and an ailing wife, could scarcely get through the week without recourse to the pawnbroker. It was their equivalent of the moneylender whose ruinous rate of interest on stockmoney crippled the costers.

When his meagre wages gave out, by Tuesday or at latest Wednesday, the poor Londoner took his one decent suit to the pawnshop. If he had no such suit his wife would take her petticoats, shoes, sheets, blanket, frying pan – whatever she had to pledge.

The decent suit, however, was as much a feature of the Londoner's self-respect as the decent Sunday dinner which gave the costers their best opportunity to make their living at the Saturday night market. The aim in life of costers and workers was identical: 'To bring somefink 'ome for the kids and put a Sunday dinner on the table'. Poor Londoners and costers were linked together in an economic stranglehold. They depended totally on one another for their livelihood. Neither could survive without the other. In bad times they went under together.

Wages were paid late on Saturday night, often in the local pub, which remained open till midnight on Saturday. The ritual procedure was for the worker, on receipt of his wages, to hurry round to the pawnshop before closing time and there redeem his Sunday suit. Then, he and his wife would rush to the night market to buy their Sunday dinner, relieved that their honour was saved for the weekend.

Not infrequently this plan miscarried. If his wages were paid out too late the worker would find the pawnshop closed. Sometimes his decent suit would be too threadbare for the pawnbroker to accept as a pledge. Often the warmth and comfort of the pub would be too much for the man, and he would linger there until he had drunk most of his wages.

Typical of this period is the worried wife anxiously pulling her husband by the sleeve to coax him out of the pub before his wages have all been spent. Phil May drew weeping little girls dragging home their intoxicated father at closing time. Songs about drunks were popular in the music halls.

Social reformers blamed the desperate poverty on drink or low wages according to their particular political views. Mission ladies preached teetotalism. Trades union leaders preached higher wages. It is typical of the period that the ebullient Marie Lloyd, when a child determined to go on stage, first appeared in public in an East End Temperance Hall where she sang a sanctimonious song about the evils of drink. She wanted a platform to display her talent and this was the only one she could get. Soon she graduated to singing in pubs, instantly dropping her teetotal turn and so on to the music halls and fame.

WEST END EPIDEMICS

The succession of epidemics (water-borne, flea-borne, rat-borne) which ravaged the slums and threatened to spread to the West End was traced to the appalling housing of the East End. 'Underground cellars, where 16 people slept' – 'Rows of back-to-back tenements constructed by speculative builders with the bricks laid narrowside to save money resulting in the collapsing of the flimsy roofs' – 'No water or sanitation of any kind included in new buildings' – 'Broken pumps in communal courts' – 'Many people with no roof over their heads sleeping on streets, in doorways and on benches, entirely without sanitation' – were reported by diligent commissions, but whatever tentative legislation to control this situation came up in Parliament, it was ignored. Neither the Tory nor the Liberal Party at that period was prepared to attack the landlords responsible.

The Mansion House did indeed set up a Council for the Dwellings of the Poor and solicited subscriptions and donations. Leading this charitable effort was the Dowager Lady Lawrence who contributed the sum of one guinea. The mission-minded ladies, however, hesitated to

'Camden Town during the Depression' – a lithograph by the author dating from 1935. The street musician, the coster flower-vendor, the children in the gutter, the unemployed man collecting cigarette ends – these were the common sights of London's poorer areas over many generations.

FEMALE PILLS FROM 8/-

STAMAROIDS! ENERGISE INVIGORATE

YOUR RUPT

Pearl Binder
1935

concern themselves with so materialistic an undertaking, and there were anxious consultations with their spiritual leaders, one of whom replied reassuringly that 'The ladies need not fear that the spiritual work will be hindered or omitted. The conversion of a privy into a proper water-closet will not disturb the conversion of souls'.

COSTERS & THEIR HOSPITALS

The London slum-dwellers had close ties with the local hospitals. Since Florence Nightingale had set them up the London hospitals' service to the poor never ceased, and the poor were grateful. Unlike the harsh reception they dreaded at the workhouse, when they were in trouble, they knew they would be treated with humanity at the hospitals.

Apart from industrial and traffic accidents and the illnesses due to malnutrition and exposure to bitter weather, the hospitals of the East End had to tackle epidemics which frequently swept through the East End slums (cholera, typhoid, small-pox etc.).

It seems miraculous that the great London hospitals, overworked, understaffed and financed only on a voluntary basis, survived at all. They depended on fund-raising by an annual 'society' dinner, bequests, and an antiquated system of appointing a legion of honorary 'Governors' (for a year or for life according to their donations) who in turn for their donations were entitled to hand out 'letters of admission' to the hospitals to patients of their choice. East End factory owners found it paid them to become a Governor in order to get speedy treatment for employees suffering illness or accident, and so keep them on their feet.

The London Hospital in Whitechapel in an effort to raise funds hired out its semi-trained nurses to private cases at two guineas a day. This caused still worse shortage of hospital staff but brought in a little regular cash.

The masses of 'sick poor' and the self-employed who suffered accident had no way of obtaining letters of admission. Such patients the hospitals accepted free, and they rapidly outnumbered the other patients. Though the hospitals never intended and were not constructed to take cholera or typhoid cases, they were forced to do so during the big epidemics.

Chronically short of space, short of trained nurses and short of funds, the London hospitals battled on. Dockers and costers were particularly prone to accidents and pulmonary diseases and it was they who eagerly joined in the regular hospital fund-raising parades. It was, in fact, their

74

determination to help their hospitals which launched the London Pearlies.

The hospitals regularly sent out 'Carnivals' to collect money in East End streets. These were fancy-dress processions ('Rags') in which medical students and nurses and junior doctors also took part. Photographs which have been preserved from the 1890s and 1900s show the internes in their white overalls and the nurses in long aprons, stiff collars and tiny caps, together with cockney helpers in crude home-made fancy costumes (Red Indian, clowns, comic policeman, Buffalo Bill etc.) assembled at the hospital with their collecting boxes ready for the parade.

The costers (expert at 'taking the basin round') enjoyed dressing-up, playing lively music and doing a turn for the carnivals. It was an extension of their mutually helpful everyday lives.

2.

The
PEARLIES

BIRTH OF THE PEARLIES

The need for fund-raising to help the hospitals had already brought into being several provident clubs and societies of poor Londoners both north and south of the Thames. Some of these clubs were religious in inspiration – some temperance. Others were neither and met in pubs. But all had the same objective – money-raising for the hospitals. Chief amongst these clubs were the Jolliboys (wet) and the Sons of Phoenix (dry). Members of these clubs used to turn out every weekend in fancy dress with their collecting boxes and join in every hospital carnival. The move over from membership of these early clubs to the later more glamorous Pearlies was simple. Such a man was Fred Tinsley who began with the Jolliboys and became the first Pearly King of Southwark. Since Coster Royalty were the outstanding and most influential costers, it was naturally they who took a leading part in these processions.

The Pearlies were well established by 1886 when, as already noted, the term is first recorded. Pearl buttons, fashionable in the West End at this period of buttoned bodices, waistcoats, long gloves and buttoned boots, had become a craze in East London life. Their sheen and glitter took the place of jewellery for poor Londoners. They became a cult. They were cheap to buy and made a handsome show. By 1890 there were two hundred factories in London alone producing pearl buttons for this voracious market. They were made from the shells of English river and tidal shell-fish shells which costers maintained were more gleaming and stronger in quality than the imported Japanese pearl buttons, now beginning to arrive in huge quantities from the Far East.

Dressy costers were quick to border the lapels and pockets of their jackets and waistcoats with pearl buttons. One young coster artfully sewed a border of pearl buttons round the hems of his bell-bottomed trousers. Another extended the buttons down the side-seams of his trousers. Coster caps glittered like crowns. Coster girls ornamented the edges of their fashionable ostrich-feathered hats with pearl buttons and sewed a close line down the front of their tight bodices. Pearl button embroidery began to appear in the carnivals, when the costers joined the procession. Having found pearly trimming a good selling gimmick on their rounds, they now realized that it was also a splendid advertisement for the hospital collection. There was and is magic in the 'flashies', as costers called their buttons, and in the movement an irridescent shimmer like a mermaid's tail.

HENRY CROFT

In July 1974 Selfridges, for a short season, mounted a 'Cockney Museum'. Amongst much that was meretricious, some authentic Pearly costumes and authentic photographs of East London brought stark reality into a commercial exercise.

It was, however, not a coster but a roadsweeper named Henry Croft who invented Pearly dress proper. In the Spring of 1974 Henry Croft's original Pearly dress was found in an old suitcase in an attic in Romford and identified by his daughter. It dates from about 1880 and is made of heavy brown woollen material in a checked pattern with a collared waistcoat and flared trousers. It had been lavishly bordered and starred with smoked pearl buttons.

Croft was less than five feet tall, shorter than his broom. An orphan brought up in an orphanage, he dedicated his life to helping the poor. As municipal roadsweeper of St Pancras markets he had a steady job and became friendly with the St Pancras costers. One particular stall especially influenced him – where two costers regularly set aside a proportion of their earnings for charity. Soon Croft was taking part in the carnivals. Like all short men he needed to draw attention to himself and he was enamoured of the costers' pearl buttons. Warm-hearted and ingenious, he lives in Pearly memory in his 'smother outfit', a worn-out dress coat, waistcoat, trousers, boots and top hat and stick from a slop-shop meticulously covered with pearl buttons. The effect of this shimmering creation in the carnivals was stupendous, the delighted onlookers pouring everything they had into his collecting box. Pearly dress had made its grand entrance.

Henry Croft did not drink or smoke (rare amongst manual workers at that time), though he collected money for charity in the pubs. He was extrovert, a good organiser, skilful with his fingers, persistent and courageous – a man of resource and tenacity. He had twelve children, lost a son in the First World War, and an adored little grand-daughter. None of his children, however, continued his work after his death.

He was much loved and respected by the costers in his lifetime and lives on in Pearly history (he died in 1930) as their honoured founder. It is reckoned that he collected over £5000 in his lifetime (by todays' value £200,000), an incredibly large amount to collect in the very small change of the slums. All he collected came from the poor for the benefit of the poor.

He was a social reformer by conviction and an early supporter of the women's suffrage movement.

Early Pearly dress is 'smothered' – following the success of Henry Croft's imaginative dress coat. His smother Pearly dress was almost the heaviest ever worn – a voluntary calvary – and the heroic effort needed by so small a man to sustain such a glittering burden for miles of marching and larking in the street carnivals, was well understood and appreciated by the onlookers, themselves labourers. The costers elected him first Pearly King of Somerstown and one of his Royal Pearly jackets was inscribed 'World King of the Pearlies'.

In his lifetime he saw the Pearlies begin and quickly spread to every London Borough, and when he died at the height of their glory Cockney London gave him a superb 'send off' and 'did him proud'. Four hundred Pearlies – every one of them in full regalia – followed his coffin in decorated donkey carts, with banners, flowers and feathers, and bagpipes, in one of the most splendid popular funerals London has ever known and which is still talked about.

PEARLY CHARITY

The first generation of Pearlies were all, like Henry Croft, sociable forceful people, without education, acutely aware of the desperate poverty around them, for they lived with it and were themselves part of it. Like Henry Croft they knew what kind of charity needed to be organised, to whom it should be offered and, almost more important, how it should be offered. They were determined to raise money and dispense it, like Henry Croft did, in the true cockney spirit – good-heartedly and with panache. No recipient of their charity was ever going to be made to feel humiliated. 'London Pride' is a flower and also an attitude to life. That attitude is what the Pearlies wanted to safeguard.

The carnivals hardly ventured outside their own neighbourhoods. All the money they collected in their boxes came from their own local people. It was self-help on a large and well organised scale, and essential to the operation was the cockney etiquette of providing good entertainment when asking for donations. Dickens died too soon to know the Pearlies whom he would certainly have loved.

A COCKNEY FOLK ART

Amongst the many legends which have grown up round the Pearlies is the one concerned with their origin. Many Pearlies believe that the fashion did not start until (in the 1880s) a Japanese cargo ship laden with pearl buttons foundered in the Thames during a fog, when its pearly cargo was washed ashore, like a gift from heaven, into the hands of the costers gambling on the wharves behind the barges. A variation of this story is that the Japanese cargo ship was seized for some excise infringement and its cargo seized and sold off cheaply, the costers being ready customers.

It was but one step to unite London regional Royalty with the Pearly cult and that step was taken in the 1880s with the election of Henry Croft to the first Pearly Kingship of Somerstown. A new, totally cockney, folk-art had begun.

All these Pearlies were poor, uneducated and talented. Though immense numbers of pearl buttons, even at fourpence a gross, could become expensive for them, they flung themselves into the exacting task of making their own theatrical glittering regalia.

Henry Croft's amazing pearled dress coat was the perfect expression of cockney sentiment at that particular moment in cockney history – the period of 'Burlington Bertie from Bow'. Against the background of drab industrial streets, the shimmering travesty of the wealthy West End man-about-town was irresistible. It was piercingly appropriate that a poor roadsweeper should transmute the West End gentleman's conventional dress, which the poorest Londoners habitually wore fifth- or sixth-hand, into a comic glory which outdid the finest real West End gentleman. In particular the top hat, unique mark of the English gentleman of the 19th century, battered beyond recognition in its journey down the social ladder and commonly worn by dockers and street mendicants, was thus raised by Henry Croft to the topmost height of impudent glory.

MUSIC HALLS & PEARLIES

The costers, born natural entertainers, were a vital part of London music hall life – as audience, publicists, inventors of songs and gags and often actual performers.

They were part and parcel of that lively cockney world of Marie Lloyd, pre-Hollywood Charlie Chaplin (both of whose parents were professional singers and who as a hungry South London child had himself once tried his luck as a coster), part of the cockney-clown world of Fred Karno whose 'mumming birds' launched Chaplin, Laurel and Hardy and so many of these English clowns who inspired America's early Keystone comedies.

The Karno music hall played to the London poor, translating their own harsh and insecure daily lives into brilliant slapstick. Fred Karno knew exactly what he was doing, for he had himself, like other cockney starvelings, scraped around for a living as plumber's mate, window-cleaner, errand boy, coster, acrobat in ramshackle travelling circuses, and barker in flea-bitten fairs.

Queen of the East End, Kate Carney, with her coster song 'Three Pots a Shilling' was the idol of the Pearlies. The three pots of flowers are still sewn as symbols on many Royal Pearly garments.

The links between music hall entertainers and their audience were very strong and intimate. Anyone, male or female, in the audience could make it on to the stage if they had it in them. And there was immense talent to be tapped in East London.

Like Charlie Chaplin, like both his parents, like so many of the great names of music hall, aspirants began by singing in pubs to a tough, highly-critical cockney audience. The fact that both performers and audience were largely illiterate only sharpened their other faculties. Cockneys demanded good tunes, witty backchat, double meanings, telling gestures, all firmly rooted in their daily lives and work. The best

lyrics were often laboriously scrawled on the back of crumpled envelopes amongst the beer-glasses. What proved to be immortal tunes whistled their way into the pubs by illiterate composers who knew nothing of 'music' and certainly could not write down the notes they whistled.

The art of working-class London was the music hall and the music halls were simply extensions of the cockney pubs. By 1900 at least 250,000 Londoners went nightly to London's four hundred music halls. The inimitable comic-nostalgic patriotic songs of this period were peculiarly British, peculiarly cockney. They were concerned with beer, food, the pitfalls of domesticity, the deflating of pretentiousness, distrust of the police, tramps, mothers-in-law and the glorification of British soldiers and sailors.

The songs the cockneys liked best were belted out with a strongly accented beat and a raucous chorus in which they could all join. Every Pearly could do a turn and play some kind of instrument. As in Mayhew's time they were skilled performers on jew's harps, tin whistles, melodeons, tea-pots, fiddles, combs and spoons.

Mrs Rebecca Matthews, first Pearly Queen of Hampstead, remembered in her old age how the girls working in the hand-laundry in her youth used to teach each other the verses of the latest music hall songs as they ironed and goffered the dozens of starched frilled aprons. Their favourite song, 'Are We to Part Like this, Bill?'.

Important to note that no love-songs were sung. The genuine coster love-songs are 'Down the Road' (about a pony), and 'Three Pots a Shilling' (about earning a living), 'My Little Boy' (still sung by old cockney women in the East End) is about making ends meet. Albert Chevalier's sentimental songs about costers and donahs were written largely for the West End. He was a professional actor with an eye on the lucrative Mayfair drawing-rooms.

Entertaining as were the comic carnival characters which by now included big-head policemen flourishing huge batons, Red Indians, clowns, pantomime comic cooks throwing dough at each other, and stilt

Mr and Mrs Bert Matthews, First Pearly King and Queen of Hampstead, in gala regalia Pearly dress. She has discarded the coster girl's white apron, insignia of her trade. They both wear the fashionable dress of the day, lavishly trimmed with pearl buttons. In the early 1900s when this photograph was taken the dress had not yet fossilised.

walkers who collected money from second-storey windows, it was the Pearlies who always stole the applause.

What Henry Croft did with his inspired zany Pearly dress was simply to bring the music hall out into the streets and use it to collect money for charity.

THE DOCKERS' STRIKE

The dazzling success of the Pearlies must be seen against the historic events of the East End at that period of Pearly beginnings. It was the time of the famous dockers' strike of 1889 'for the docker's tanner' (6d a day). Dock work was casual and there was much unemployment.

In summer the dockers slept rough as they could rarely afford a 'penny sit-up'. They lived on what scraps of food they could find, such as waste spoiled rice thrown from cargo ships, which was free because no-one wanted it. In winter they tried to spend the nights under a roof in the twopenny doss-houses.

The dock strike began without funds for there were none. Will Thorne (later Member of Parliament for Plaistow) who had never gone to school because he was working in a rope factory from the age of six to support himself and his sick mother, tried to organise some practical help for the dockers' children who were starving.

Thorne, illiterate till the age of 25 when he was taught to read by Karl Marx's daughter Eleanor, went round the Saturday night markets in Canning Town begging bones from the butchers and vegetable scraps from the costers. These he boiled into soup in a cauldron on Sunday morning in the open to keep the Canning Town children alive.

Contributions to the strikers came in farthings and halfpence from their own people (amongst them costers and Pearlies) and finally a handsome donation of £30,000 from Australian trades unionists enabled the dockers to hold out long enough to win. These Australians had been unemployed London dockers whom the English Dockers' Union had assisted to emigrate.

Forty years later, in the 1930s, when the unemployed Welsh miners walked to London to sing in the streets, the Pearlies collected money to keep them alive whilst they put their case to Parliament. Mementos from this undertaking, in the shape of miniature miners' lamps, are still treasured in Pearly Royal families.

Nevertheless the Pearlies themselves remained non-political. During the period of working-class ferment which finally transformed the many

84

Albert Chevalier, the singer of sentimental songs about costers, in his full coster stage costume. This photograph dates from the days when the pearl button rage was just beginning – the period of the Phil May drawings of East End life – in the early 1890s.

little provident societies into the Labour Party, the Pearlies took no part. They were sympathetic to its ideals and aims for costers themselves suffered severely from the lack of a trades union.

But they felt their Pearly task to be of a different nature. They were artists and their rôle was to help the needy by 'taking the basin round'.

PEARLY PATTERNS

The original 'smother' concept was so to cover the material with closesewn pearl buttons that no glimpse of the stuff showed through. The weight of this smother style was extremely heavy. The 60,000 pearl buttons needed to sew all over a complete Royal suit could weigh three-quarters of a cwt. Some of these original smother garments have survived and are still worn today.

It was not only the heavy weight of total 'smother' Pearly dress which brought about a change of style, but also the need for public declaration of Pearly Royal territories. Election to Royal rank was the old rule and once elected the Pearly Royal had the duty to proclaim his realm and the extent of his territories. This was achieved by a statement of Royal rank and realm outlined in pearl buttons on the back of the jacket or waistcoat. Elsewhere on the Royal garments the buttons were used to make splendid patterns, rich borders and curious symbols.

From the beginning the need to differentiate, no less than Pearly pride in originality, impelled each Pearly Royal to work out individual patterns for his own regalia, which he had to sew himself. So too did his wife. So too did Royal Pearly children as soon as they were old enough.

In the making of Royal Pearly dress, the requisites for the production of works of art were all present. The medium itself was difficult but enchanting. The sphere to be worked on was limited and highly personal, manual skills and patience were essential, and there was the reassurance of an appreciative public to understand and admire when the work was completed. They were not working for money nor for a boss but for their own delight. No artist could wish for better terms.

As in other fields of art, cross-fertilisations and metamorphoses soon took place. Fred Tinsley (a real coster) was influenced by the coster stage-dress of Albert Chevalier, an actor. Tinsley also was inspired by a crown he observed in a shop window. Henry Croft himself was inspired to create his own smother Pearly suit by a music hall comedian who covered his stage-dress with shining brass buttons. But no Pearly could copy the patterns of any other Pearly.

The first Pearlies favoured large bold patterns. Later smaller patterns were preferr᠉d. Some Pearlies have fancied mixing large and small buttons. Others have developed negative patterns by leaving the required pattern unstiched and filling in the background with pearl buttons.

This photograph of a carnival about to go collecting for a hospital is the first recorded camera study of the Pearlies at work. Mr and Mrs Bert Matthews (left) in Pearly dress amongst other masquers – Red Indians, Buffalo Bills, Hungarian, sailor, jockey, etc. The hospital nurses and internes accompanied these early carnivals which have survived in the form of the charity-collecting student rags of today. Circa 1900.

The Pearly costume of Mr Pomeroy (Pearly King of Kentish Town, a donkey-owning coster), was mushroom-coloured in a check pattern, bordered with red velvet and close-sewn with pearl buttons – amongst them a scattering of small red buttons (known as 'red bugs'). His Pearly cap had a tassel of pearl beads. He also had a pearled whip.

Mrs Pomeroy's Pearly Queen outfit was navy blue serge with a red velvet hat, close-sewn with pearl buttons (red, white and blue ensemble) and her shoes were pearled.

Mr Hall (Pearly King of Willesden, a flower-seller), only used thin flat mother-of-pearl, sewn in meticulously with white croched cotton. He worked from cardboard templates.

William Golden (Pearly King of Woolwich) made one Pearly suit of grey chalk-striped material with black trousers. The coat was sewn with a motto in buttons, ALL FOR CHARITY, also patterns of rosettes, horse-shoes, three pots a shilling, rayed suns, cardinal-pointed crosses, and old boots. He wore a pearled cap, pearled bow tie, and pearled walking stick.

Bert Lodge (Pearly King of the Borough), 40 years in buttons, claimed the innovation of using red thread which showed up well on the pearl buttons.

Mr Montague (Pearly King of Stonebridge Park) used a design on his Pearly dress he had copied from the glass door of a public house.

Alfred Meader (Pearly King of Hackney) embroidered the three feathers ensign of the Prince of Wales in large pearl buttons on his jacket and included a touch of gold paint on some of the buttons, knotting each button on separately. This outfit took him seven and a half months to complete. Mrs Meader's Pearly Queen dress used bugle beads (red, white and green sewn in triangles).

Harry Springfield (Pearly King of Stoke Newington) used all tinted buttons dyed with Drummer dyes.

Bill Davidson (Pearly King of West Ham, later Newham) an old docker and soldier made the most beautiful regalia in harlequin triangles of tinted small pearl buttons – last of several spectacularly handsome outfits, each different. His dog Rover had his own Pearly blanket with the motto—ALL FOR CHARITY. He had a pearly cap, pipe and spectacles and Bill taught him to bark a thank-you for contributions.

The balance of the whole Pearly dress was a delicate individual matter achieved by artistic decision and carried out by careful measur-

A famous Pearly Queen at home: Mrs Fred Tinsley,
Pearly Queen of Southwark, rests her feet and
enjoys a glass of stout.
Regalia patterns on her costume include butterflies, domino squares, eyes of God, spirals.
1960.

ing, often by sleight of hand and trust in the judgement of the eyes alone. Some Pearlies made elaborate templates. Others sewed their buttons straight on. Others again drew their designs in white chalk which they folded over and rubbed on to the opposite half of the dress. No Pearly dress was ever completed without at least three months' hard work. It was a matter of pride that each Pearly designed and made his own Pearly dress. But some Pearlies sewed their wives' buttons for them, and vice versa. Pearly designs are fanciful, luck-orientated, often deeply pagan.

Borders (age-old protection from evil) are usually close-set.

Good luck signs, such as horse-shoes, crosses, old boots, ace of spades, diamonds, hearts and clubs.

Fertility symbols such as stars, suns, moons, flowers, cups, spirals, teapots.

Magic protective/demon-scaring: The lozenge-shaped 'eye of God', flying birds, Faith, Hope and Charity (cross anchor and heart), bells, 'Bow bells', knots, crowns, firework rockets.

Job protection: Historic versions of the costers' song 'Three Pots a Shilling', and stylised donkey carts with coster and donkey.

The circle motif frequently appears. It symbolises the sun, the wheel of fortune, the wheels of the donkey cart, money, eternity and Big Ben's face.

Pearlies cannot say (except that they 'fancied' them) exactly why they choose the designs they sew on their dresses. But it is fascinating that peasant people all over the world traditionally choose similar patterns for the ornamentation of their garments.

Triple and waxed button-hole thread was usually employed to sew on the buttons. Some fancied red thread. Later nylon thread was introduced.

Pearlies are skilled in producing damask effects by overlapping and the clever use of pearl buttons on patterned material and different colours and kinds of material.

PEARLY FASHIONS

Male fashions have changed so little that the earliest Pearly suits do not look unfashionable today. Indeed the waistcoat, cap, kingsman and bell-bottomed trousers of the Pearly Princes is today again the height of fashion.

The dress of Pearly Queens fossilised about 1900. The fashion of that period was for enormous cartwheel hats, swept by ostrich feathers, a tight-waisted flared jacket worn over a white blouse, and a ground-length tulip-shaped skirt with the fullness at the back. The feathered hat and blouse have been retained.

The concept of a coat and skirt has also been retained, though the length of skirt changes today with the current fashion. There have been Pearly mini-skirts worn with the cartwheel feathered hats.

Usually Pearly Royal women choose a richly pearled dark suit and white blouse. The Pearly Queen of Peckham, Mrs Major, and her Pearly Princesses, Janet, Tammy, Kim and Yvonne,* wore brown, pearled with white, at the 1973 Harvest Festival Service. Jewellery, especially pearls, is worn with Pearly dress. Heavy sparkling earrings look very handsome framed by the great hat which is often decorated with buttons outlining the brim. Pearled parasols were carried on excursions and pearled handbags are carried today. There is no limit to the number of ostrich feathers which may be worn. The choice of colours, too, is left to the wearer, but by tradition, patriotic red, white and blue feathers are preferred. Lupino Lane's coster wife sported 27 ostrich feathers in her cartwheel hat.

In the 90 years since the Pearlies began variations have developed. There was the curious innovation of 'red bugs', small red bead-like buttons, or red beads, introduced into the male dress in small numbers, especially in the decoration of the cap. Purists do not care for them, but 'red bugs' are now also a tradition. Tinted pearl buttons have found their way in. These are dyed at home. The impossibility of obtaining good pearl buttons (or indeed any kind of pearl buttons) today has given the Pearlies much anxiety. They hate to use plastic buttons, and yet must continually replace pearl buttons which get lost or broken off or pulled off by admirers. In recent times a few Pearlies have chosen to wear a tie (suitably embroidered with pearl buttons) instead of a kingsman.

PEARLIES & DONKEYS

An important part of the Pearly way of life was the donkey-cart. It was the dream of every coster girl and youth to acquire a donkey, set up together young, and start off on their own. To save up for a donkey they took on all sorts of extra work (even in the hated factories) and worked

*Bill Davidson helped prepare their costumes, worked in a variation of his distinctive harlequin pattern.

long extra hours. There were tempting 'donkey raffles' at threepence, fourpence or even sixpence a number, and some lucky coster might acquire a donkey cheaply in unusual circumstances.

John Marriott the third told me that as a youth he found out that at the closing of the Lyceum pantomime their stage donkey would be going for sale cheap. He hurried to the Lyceum and bargained with the stage manager. When he had succeeded in buying the donkey (a beautiful little beast named Polly, in excellent condition), the stage manager warned him never to tap her rump and say 'Gee-up', as she had been performing a trick on stage which involved her instantly sitting down and refusing to move on hearing those words. Mr Marriott was too excited to ask for the counter sign word.

On his triumphant way back to Finsbury with Polly harnessed to her cart, Mr Marriott got involved in the tramlines amongst heavy horse-traffic near Kings Cross (drays, cabs, tramcars, etc. and some early upright motor cars). Forgetting the warning, he smote Polly on the rump and shouted the fatal words 'Gee-up!' Polly, obedient to her training, at once sat down and refused to budge. Nothing could get her to her feet again, and the fire-brigade (horse-drawn) had to be sent for and Polly and the cart bodily lifted in. Thus her proud but embarrassed new owner arrived back in Finsbury to start his career as a donkey-owning young coster.

Once he had a donkey and cart the coster could set-up for himself. He now had transport. He was freed from the strain of pushing twelve hundredweight of vegetables about London and could venture further afield when he chose. He had individual transport at a time when transport was beyond the reach of poor people. Now, not only was the Pearly family dressed up in Pearly dress on festival occasions, but the donkey, donkey blanket and the whip could also be decorated with pearl buttons. The Sunday outing now became an event. On special occasions the family in their Pearly dress (with every button polished) and disposed on a handsomely pearled blanket behind the well-groomed donkey, went bowling along to Richmond or Kew or Greenwich for a day's pleasure, to the admiration of everybody on the way.

Epsom and Derby were now within reach and the Pearlies made the most of them.

'It used to take seven hours by donkey-cart', recalls Mrs Marriott 'then five hours by pony-cart and today – oh well, there's the motor car'.

Fairs were never complete without Pearly families shaking their collecting tins. At Kensal Rise fair, a popular Pearly occasion, there were special coster races with a tower of baskets balanced on the head of each coster runner, and special donkey races. Silver cups were offered for the donkey winners and for the best Pearly 'turn-out'. Immaculately groomed donkeys with shining reins and burnished brasswork, brightly painted donkey-carts crammed with the Pearly Kings and their Pearly Royal families all meticulously groomed, with pearl handbag, pearl-embroidered cart-blanket, pearled whip and pearled parasol, thrilled the crowds.

Pearly 'Helpers' added to the glitter and excitement. Costers who had not achieved the rank of donkey-owners hired donkey-carts for these occasions. Coffee-stalls, jellied-eel stalls, buns, cakes, vivid coloured soft drinks, singers, musicians, bands, floods of beer, acrobats, and all the fun of the fair enlivened these cockney fiestas.

Different but no less joyful was the annual family trek (by donkey-cart if there was one) to the Kent hop-fields for the seasonal hop-picking – a working holiday. Here, in the small huts allotted to them, the costers created their own temporary homes, bringing their own utensils and wallpapering the rough wooden clap-boards.

Weddings, whether officially sanctioned or not, were another occasion for an outing. If the weather was kind, the friends of the young couple would come along, in their donkey-carts to join in the fun, and there were frequent obligatory stops at pubs along the way. Pearlies added to the importance and colour of the occasion and were sure to get a good collection.

Front and back views of the Pearly regalia of Mr
F. Bliss, Pearly King of Islington.
Bliss was a 'loner' and there was never a Pearly Queen to share his Royal task. The regalia is of a very early cut, possibly the 1880s, with a short jacket displaying embroidered flies to the trousers which fasten at the sides, many pockets and a fancy waistcoat.
Pearly patterns include playing-cards, rosettes, four-leaved clover, the card suites of hearts, diamonds, clubs and spades, rayed suns, fish, butterflies, champagne corks, horses' heads.
Circa 1888.

PEARLIES & HARVEST FESTIVALS

Harvest Festivals were peculiarly the Pearlies' and costers' special occasion. The church where they were first held was St. Mary Magdalene, Southwark, then subsequently at St Mary Magdalene's in Bermondsey. Later the south London Pearlies used Lady Margaret Church (off the New Kent Road) while north London Pearlies held their services in the church of St Martins-in-the-Fields, Trafalgar Square, which now unites all Pearlies. The costers were hardly believers in organised religion but fruit and vegetables were their lives and this was their special day, the basic Festival of Pagan Fertility.

PEARLY FUNERALS

The greatest of all Pearly occasions were funerals. No Pearly turnout could excel the dignity and splendour of the Pearly cortège on these all-important occasions. Henry Croft's funeral, as we have said, is still talked about. Those who had no donkey-cart of their own hired one. The monument on his grave shows him in his famous buttoned dress, coat and top hat. Carved marble cannot recreate the glory of the flashies, essentially concerned with the play of light on nacreous surfaces however, and unfortunately there survives no good photograph of Henry Croft in his amazing regalia – an imposing figure despite his lack of inches.

PEARLY TITLES

There were soon more Pearlies than all the London Boroughs could accommodate with Royal rank. Therefore a system grew up whereby in addition to the Pearly Royal Sovereign of a London Borough, each ward of the borough was also represented by a Pearly personality – the collective wards sponsoring a Pearly 'Pride'.

There were in addition an unlimited number of Pearly 'Helpers' who enjoyed the fun and the collecting and made their own Pearly dress but had no special rank.

Pearly work of collecting necessitated an immense amount of careful planning and organisation, every carnival being a heavy undertaking. The strictest accounting was vital. It is no small tribute to their innate intelligence and ability that the first Pearlies did so well at the practical side of their self-appointed task without all the fuss and form-filling of the later official upper-class flag days.

ORIGINAL PEARLY KING & QUEEN'S ASSOCIATION,

Headquarters Branch - KINGS CROSS. Established 1911

The Golden Lion, 2, Britannia Street, King's Cross, W.C.1.

(TEL.- STA 4725.)

Chairman Bro. P. STAY
Vice do. Bro. Springfield
Min Sec. Bro. J MARRIOTT

Founder. J MARRIOTT Senr.
Treasurer Bro. F. HALL
+:> ALL OFFICERS HONORARY. <:+

All Communications to Gen. Sec.
Sister B. MARRIOTT
2 KILLECK HOUSE,

OUR MOTTO - "ONE NEVER KNOWS"

This

This Is To Certify That Brother W. Davison Has Been Elected To

Take The Title Of Pearly King Of West Ham.

This Title Was Given And Voted By Members And Committe Of The

Above Association.

Yours Very Sincerely

_ister B. Marriott

Hon. General Secretary

The Original Pearly King And Queen On London.

Certificate of Election of Bill Davidson to the rank
of Pearly King of West Ham by the Original Pearly
King and Queen's Association in August 1929.
The mode of address is similar to that of 19th
century Trade Union usage.

97

The Pearlies

PEARLY KINGS & QUEENS ASSOCIATION

In 1910 John Marriott, second Pearly King of Finsbury, husband of Beatrice Marriott who acted as its secretary, founded the Pearly Kings and Queens Association which was distinct from Fred Tinsley's former smaller Pearly Guild. Fred Tinsley was Pearly King of Southwark and his Guild covered South London. John Marriott was Pearly King of Finsbury and his Association covered North London.

The Association met in the Golden Lion pub in Britannia Street, Kings Cross, and issued a simple form of membership document to elected members. Their name was The Helping Hand, their motto 'You Never Know'.

It is true to say the Pearlies were fatalists. But they were also optimists. The recurrent and favourite circular motif on their Pearly dress may symbolise the sun, or the wheel of their donkey-cart, but it is also the wheel of fortune, and they saw no reason not to hope, in traditional coster style, that it could turn, if they faced life bravely, in their favour.

WEAR & TEAR OF PEARLY COSTUME

The Pearlies, most of them costers, took the immense physical effort of the costers' work into their charity work. Pushing a twelve cwt. loaded barrow is good training for carrying the immense weight of a fully-pearled Pearly costume. Extremely hot to wear, rigid as armour, Pearly dress is difficult and awkward to move about in. Rain ruins it. The cost of keeping it up is heavy, and later when pearl buttons became unobtainable, replacement impossible.

Pearlies dye and curl their ostrich feathers themselves, dye their own tinted pearl buttons at home, and of course design and sew their Pearly dress themselves. But they cannot make the actual pearl buttons.

Some Pearlies are reluctantly obliged to introduce plastic buttons to fill the gaps. Some introduce jewels that glitter. Harry Tongue (Pearly King of Tottenham) has bordered his Pearly cap with a pearl necklace.

Every time Pearly dress is worn Pearlies complain that some of the buttons get broken or lost and must be replaced. Besides this people believe these traditional pearl buttons to be lucky and beg for one, 'Give us a button, Pearly!', or stealthily break one off for themselves. After the Second World War the WVS helped collect pearl buttons to repair the war ravages when many Pearly costumes were lost in the bombing raids. In 1974 an appeal from BBC TV's *Jackanory* children's

Mrs Tolhurst (Pearly Queen of Walworth) furbishing
her Pearly regalia for the first post-war costers'
parade at St Mary Magdalene's Church in Southwark, October 1947. Her daughter Betty is helping
her.

The war had damaged and eroded Mrs Tolhurst's
costume, many pearl buttons were missing and
almost impossible to replace even at 6d each. Her
ostrich plumes were newly cleaned and re-curled.

programme brought a welcome shower but the Pearlies are still desperately short of pearl buttons.

The upkeep of Pearly dress is always costly and time-consuming. Few Pearlies today have the necessary extra Pearly dress and a good Pearly never goes out in his regalia without meticulously polishing every button.

PEARLIES TODAY

We began this book by asking who the Pearlies are. We must end by asking what of their future?

If, as is unhappily the case, the Pearlies are declining in numbers today, we must seek the reasons.

1. Has the Welfare State taken away the need for charity?

Absolutely not. Every hospital needs far more than the National Health Service can provide. The orphanages, the crippled children, the paraplegics, the blind babies, the old people, and dozens more worthy causes also all need help and entertainment.

2. Do London Boroughs still keep up their Pearly Royalty?

London itself is changing fast. Elizabeth I's 'great wen' is daily growing more enormous. New boroughs are being created which stretch deep into Essex, Middlesex and Surrey, and other new boroughs are created by cannibalising or rejigging old London Boroughs. New Pearly Kings and Queens are needed for new areas but the two world wars have seriously decimated the Pearly Kings and Princes and broken up old Pearly dynasties. There has been a cruel loss both of boundaries and personalities. Once every London Borough had its elected Pearly Royal family and its non-Royal Pearly Pride of helpers, as integral a part of the civic set-up as the Mayor and Corporation. Today many London Boroughs have no Pearly Royalty. Some London Boroughs which incorporate several older ones are now represented only by elderly Pearly Royal widows or widowers whose descendants are no longer interested in the duties and pageantry of Pearly life. Or they may have no descendants. Some Pearly lines have simply died out for lack of heirs. Some old Pearly Royals have moved right out of London into retirement, and they cannot be replaced.

There are no longer plenty of Pearlies from whom to elect the most suitable to Royal status. Because the Pearlies are so short of males today, when there is no direct heir they are glad to recruit new Pearly Royalty outside the legitimate lineage – unthinkable in the early days.

Candidates for the thrones are not easy to find today. London is more affluent. The urge to tackle unpaid charity work has diminished. The heavy unpaid duties and necessary Pearly Royal qualities (strong personality, physical toughness, manual dexterity, ready wit and cheerful exhibitionism) do not altogether tally with today's image of the likely young Londoner.

High-rise blocks of municipal flats and privately owned offices, supermarkets, ring-roads and car parks have changed the face of London. Pearly Royalty have lost their former cottages and their coster stables. Old Mrs Marriott, rehoused in a municipal flat, comments: 'It's a lodging not a living'.

The old London street markets were like fairs. People stopped and chatted, exchanged jokes and dropped their small change in the Pearly's box at their leisure. Today everyone is in a hurry. The supermarkets of today are mechanised. The human touch is absent. London street-life, once so rich and entertaining, is vanishing.

3. What is happening to Pearly dress?

Amazingly, some of the original Pearly outfits are still in existence and still worn. John Marriott, the fourth Pearly King of Finsbury, a youth, has inherited the original totally pearled suit of his grandfather. It is much too heavy for him to wear. Wiggy Marriott (Pearly King of Lambeth) still wears handsomely pearled regalia trousers which are forty-seven years old. Rose Matthews Smith (Pearly Queen of Camden) has a magnificent collection of her parents' Pearly regalia. These heirlooms are carefully looked after and mended and passed down the family. Highly individual with title and territory blazoned on the back, Pearly dress, properly and proudly passed down to rightful heirs, cannot be transferred to other Royals of other territories. Pearlies hate destroying a beautiful old Pearly dress by taking off the buttons to make a new dress, but sometimes they have to.

The handsomest and earliest embroideries were sometimes worked on to almost threadbare garments and have deteriorated with the garments. When old fashioned haberdashers close down today there is a Pearly rush to salvage their ancient boxes of real pearl buttons.

Pearly Queens, while clinging to the feathered cartwheel hat of the 1890s like to wear their skirts the fashionable length so that they are always having to remake their skirts, and without real pearl buttons it is a dispiriting task. Pearly children soon outgrow their Pearly dress and often there is no Pearly outfit waiting to be inherited. Today's Pearly children are bigger than their ancestors. Mrs Beatrice Marriott has been indefatigable (for over fifty years) in collecting, dyeing and curling ostrich feathers, and finding and tinting pearl buttons. The St Martins-in-the-Fields Harvest Festival Pearly Service in 1973 was attended by only fourteen Pearlies. But all had taken enormous pains with their costumes, several of which were newly made.

Some Pearly costumes, or parts of costumes, have found their way into private collections and into museums both here and in Australia and America. Parts of Pearly regalia sometimes come up for auction. And, sadly, some ageing Pearlies have been tricked out of their priceless costumes by cunning speculators. The real Pearlies detest this trafficking. What they have worked on for love and for charity they feel should not be commercialised.

Many superstitions as we have seen have accumulated round Pearly dress. I was recently assured by a middle-class lady in Brighton who had never met a Pearly that each button on a Pearly's dress indicated that the Pearly had £100 in the bank.

Most people who enjoy looking at the Pearlies, have no idea what the dress means. In the ordinary way they see Pearlies only face-to-face. They never see the back of the Pearly Royal dress with its territorial claims. There is a magic moment during the Pearly Harvest Festival Service in St Martins-in-the-Fields, when the Pearly Kings and Pearly Princes, having taken the collection, perform a group right-about-turn and march to the altar with their offerings. Then it is that Pearly heraldry, its titles and territories and its whole raison d'être are truly revealed, and Pearly history is suddenly illuminated in a flush of pearls.

4. How do Pearlies get along with one another?

Like Royal royalty, they have had their battles of lineage, their rivalries and war of protocol. At the death of Bert Matthews, original Pearly King of Hampstead, his son Edward was unmarried. His daughter Rose (senior in age to Edward and married to a coster named George Smith) claimed the throne for herself and her husband. This claim was disputed by other Pearly Royals who said Edward should have inherited. Rose, however, prevailed and is now indisputably Pearly Queen of Camden (once Hampstead) and her husband George is

The Christening of a Pearly baby in the Church of
St Mary Magdalene, Southwark.
Circa 1920.

Pearly Prince Consort. Rose and her husband have been cool with the
other Pearlies, though they collect faithfully for good causes and are
sent abroad on tours by the Board of Trade, being a handsome pair
with sparkling personalities and superb regalia.

A different variety of contretemps blew up when Bill Golden, Pearly
King of Woolwich, whose wife Pearly Queen Sarah had made him a
new Pearly suit, sold for £2 his old Royal Pearly regalia to Mr Alfred
West, a comic-policeman and collector. Mr West then claimed himself
to be the rightful King of Woolwich by virtue of possession of the Royal
regalia. Battle raged. John Marriott the second, leader of the London
Pearlies, was called upon to settle the claim. Verdict: 'Mr West is not a

Pearly King and never will be. Mr Golden is the one and only Pearly King of Woolwich.'

Protocol troubles have arisen from innocent good intentions. The well-meaning Mr Montague, when Pearly King of Willesden, took it upon himself to organise the collection of money to send a blind girl to a special school for the blind in Scotland. Mr Montague, in all good faith, was deceived insofar as the father of the girl turned out to be a publican of comfortable means. As the Pearlies resented Mr Montague's individual effort and misplaced zeal he afterwards preferred to organise his own collecting outside London.

Montague's experience illuminated a basic Pearly principle for which first the Pearly Guild and later the Pearly Kings and Queens Association were formed to regulate. All Pearly collecting must be made for bona fide charities, their collecting boxes must all be stamped and checked at issue, and checked at delivery when filled, and an official receipt given for the money collected. They collect for general not individual charity so as to keep malefactors at bay. Such splendid concepts as were possible in the early Pearly days (like that Dickensian collection for a Christmas dinner for one hundred old East End women, with a triumphal donkey-cart drive to the Albert Hall) are out of place today. Need they be?

Making such rigorous checks and clerical supervision as Pearlies undertake to do today ensures honesty. Pearlies are naturally indignant when bogus Pearlies turn up brazenly at street corners in London, especially round Oxford Street, to collect for themselves. Real Pearlies have their places and times arranged beforehand with the authorities, and a proper licence to collect. Real Pearlies believe the police are too casual in their apprehension of bogus Pearlies.

5. How do Pearlies get along with the police today?

Owing to the proliferation of flag days in aid of the ever-growing number of charities after the First World War, a system of licensing for street collecting was introduced by the government in 1925. The Pearlies were regarded by the authorities as just another group of charity collectors. Every Pearly was required to carry a police permit to collect, and their collecting times and places were strictly regulated. This has irritated the Pearlies considerably because they have never been just another group of charity collectors, but something more significant.

However, they have accepted these regulations and their enforcement by the police, and gone to Bow Street to get their licences with as good grace as they could muster. But the old coster dislike of the police, and the policeman's old dislike of the costers, were sharply rekindled. Pearlies saw the regulation as just another chance for the police to goad them, and they still believe that the police harrass them for their licence more than they do flag-selling society ladies.

'Pearly, where's your licence?' any policeman at any time can and does demand of a Pearly in regalia with his collecting box. The Pearly riposte (stemming back to the old coster routine in Mayhew's day with his wheelless barrow) is to put on a panic-stricken face, slowly go through every single one of his many pockets, until finally, when the policeman appears to be on the edge of losing his temper, triumphantly produce the necessary permit from some unlikely hiding place such as inside his shoe.

6. What has happened to the great Pearly dynasties?

The first generation of Pearly Royalty, though so overworked and ill-fed like Mayhew's costers, seemed eternal. Most of them lived to ripe old age. They seemed to have too much to do to have time to die. Mrs Phoebe Marriott, first Pearly Queen of Finsbury, born in 1862, lived to be 87, and her husband, Robert Henry Marriott, first Pearly King of this famous dynasty, lived well into his 70s. Mary Tinsley (first Pearly Queen of Southwark) lived to 79. Her famous husband Fred (first Pearly King of Southwark) lived still longer. Martha Morris (Pearly Queen of Bethnal Green) was going strong at the age of 85. Rebecca Matthews (first Pearly Queen of Hampstead) lived to the age of 77 and her husband still longer. Thomas Golden (Pearly King of Woolwich) lived to 80. His wife, Sarah Ann Golden (82 in 1974) having retired from active Pearly collecting is now busy making Pearly dolls at home to sell for the same charities. George Dale lived to be 85, and the Nutley Pearly family of Hoxton are having a popular revival.

There was intermarriage between the original Pearly Royal families which reinforced the dynasties. For instance, the Marriotts intermarried with the Springfields. But, as we have said, the two world wars cut cruel swathes into the Pearly Kings and Princes. Today their widows wear their photographs and war medals pinned on to their own Pearly dress. In any Pearly gathering black arm-bands are common.

Pearly Kings today find the collecting work in their heavy regalia a strain. The 63 lbs weight of young John Marriotts's inherited Royal

Preparing for the Great Pearly Ball of 1927 which
the Duke and Duchess of York (now the Queen
Mother) attended.

Pearly dress tore his muscles when he first wore it, so that he was off
work for several weeks. (Yet his grandmother, old Mrs Beatrice Marriott,
wears a completely pearled long coat and dress which weigh still more.)

Pearlies live in flats not cottages today and have fewer children.
Pearly daughters now often marry out, and if the husband (as in the
case of Jean Marriott) is not interested in the Pearlies it makes it
difficult for the girl to keep up Pearly work. Jean, however, is still a
staunch Pearly, bringing up her three O'Shea children in buttons, and

they were all christened at St Martins-in-the-Fields in the family pearled christening shawl. Mrs Marriott's grand-daughter, Pearly Queen of Wood Green (Jean's sister Linda) has married a printer named Elliott who has become a Pearly and is now Pearly King of Wood Green.

7. What about the Pearly donkeys?

The high-rise modern London has swept much away – Pearly cottages and Pearly donkey stables. Typical of the present situation: the late John Marriott (who died in 1971) was heart-broken when the developers pulled down his rented stables, and though he soon earned a better living as an electronics engineer than he did as a street coster, he mourned his old trade and way of life.

8. What were the Pearly Balls?

It was John Marriott, the first Pearly King of Finsbury, who organized the two great Pearly Balls of 1927 and 1928 at the Pithead Baths, Finsbury, for Royal Royals and Pearly Royals. The guests of honour were the Duke and Duchess of York (later King George VI and his Queen, now the Queen Mother) and Princess Marie-Louise, a grand-daughter of Queen Victoria and a particular friend and patron of the Pearlies, some of whom named their baby girls after her. Mrs Beatrice Marriott's daughter Marie-Louise (now Pearly Queen of Finsbury) is the Princess's god-daughter. Princess Marie-Louise presented John Marriott with a crimson velvet Royal Arm-Band embroidered in gold in apprecia-tion of their long years of good work for charity. The arm-band is now a treasured memento in the collection of Mrs Beatrice Marriott.

9. Are the Pearlies changing their image?

The Marriotts were successful dynastically because they had many children, grandchildren, uncles, aunts, and cousins who kept their line going and their Pearly activity alive. It is when a Pearly line becomes extinguished by death, retirement or even indifference that a borough can suddenly be left without its Pearly Royalty.

This is what happened to the Borough of Greenwich (later joined by Deptford, and then even Margate) which had no Pearly representative until a Mr and Mrs Pinaud applied to the Greenwich Borough Council for the post and the vacant throne was awarded them by the Greenwich Town Clerk.

This is totally against all precedent for they should by tradition have been elected or refused by the Pearly Kings and Queens. Moreover Mr Pinaud, though a coster at one time, was not even English but a Channel Islander, and his wife, Irish. Far from being born within the sound of Bow Bells, neither was born in England at all. Mrs Pinaud regarded her rôle as social. Her husband George, being clever with his fingers, made their regalia which was interesting but not truly in the Pearly tradition.

Mrs Kitty Pinaud thought the Pearly heartiness vulgar, and departed from Pearly tradition by introducing a special evening outfit with pearled bolero and dainty evening seed-pearled pochette. She objected to the traditional cap and coster kingsman and insisted on her husband pearling a bow tie and top hat.

There is a difference of outlook here between Henry Croft and the Pinauds which seventy years may explain. Henry Croft was guying the top hat when he covered it with pearl buttons. Mrs Pinaud insisted on a top hat as more gentlemanly than a cap.

10. Are all Pearlies cockneys?

Though the Pearlies consider themselves born and bred cockneys not all of them were born in London, certainly not east London. Henry Croft himself came from Somerstown in north London. Mrs Morris came from Sheffield; Fred Tinsley, Mr Turner and William Golden all came from Lancashire. Tinsley himself, though he became a coster, came from a Lancashire weaving family. Only Albert Singfield, the original Pearly King of Whitechapel, was truly born within the sound of Bow Bells.

11. Has the Pearly cult spread?

Pearlies are unfailingly popular overseas and on that account are included in Trade Missions. Rose Matthews-Smith and her husband George have toured Canada, Australia and Sweden. John Marriott the second and his wife Rose toured Australia and Japan. Mrs Beatrice Marriott was chosen to travel to Italy to launch the P. & O. ship *Spirit of London* (for the America–Mexico–Canada run). It was her first travel to the Continent and she was over seventy. She performed the ceremony in splendid style and greatly enjoyed herself. The Hitchens, Pearly King and Queen of the City of London, were sent by hovercraft to convey greetings to the Mayor of Brussels. Chris and Linda Elliott, Pearly King and Queen of Wood Green, though very young, toured

Beatrice and John Marriott (Second Pearly King and Queen of Finsbury), Princess Marie-Louise, and a Pearly King in drag at the Great Pearly Ball of 1927.

Brazil recently with a British Trade Mission.

In Suva (Fiji) today there is an 'All-races' Boys Club run by an Englishman, formerly an RAF boxing instructor – Harry Charman, who calls himself ''Arry Boy from Soho' – his invented title worn in pearl buttons on a home-made Pearly suit. He raises large sums of money for this club and some of his youths have become Olympic Games participants and champions.

Mrs Helen Wood, formerly Pearly Queen of Hoxton, emigrated to Southern Rhodesia some years ago and became friends with a Mrs Muteya of the Sjangaan tribe whose native dress, closely sewn with white beads, curiously resembles her own Pearly dress.

12. If the Pearly saga today shows signs of disintegration, what is the trouble?

It is most of all an attitude to life that makes a Pearly. Anything mean, humourless, genteel, snobbish, mercenary or unpatriotic is anathema to them. They are Dickensian in spirit. If this traditional image fails them they cannot survive. The miracle is that in today's world they have so far survived. Cockney culture successfully weathered (even incorporated) successive waves of immigrants throughout the 19th century. It has been unable to stand up so well against the American cultural invasion of the 20th century. And it is now struggling for its life against Common Market conformity.

Today the Pearlies, like the rest of us in England, are struggling to keep their identity.

The very process of buying food has become more of a trauma for them than for the rest of us. Costers were concerned with fresh vegetables and traditional Sunday dinners. Mrs Phoebe Marriott was still selling fresh beetroot and fresh mint from her shallow in Chapel Street market in her extreme old age (she died in 1950). Today their lively street markets, with their brisk music hall backchat, have nearly all gone. In their place are the automated plastic supermarkets silently selling a dozen varieties of ready-wrapped alien cheddar but no Cheddar cheddar – no English cheddar.

Singers and audience were one, so close to real East End London life were the old London music halls. Mrs Beatrice Marriott recalls her childhood when her coster parents took the whole family to the local music hall every Friday with a large bag of boiled sweets, a treat and an education for the children. They sang the cockney songs they learnt there till the next week when Friday night brought them a fresh cockney harvest.

The last authentic cockney song dates from the First World War – 'Ten Days Leave' (it brings in the cinema as 'the pictures'). It was still sung by the Pearlies' idol, Kate Carney, when she was over 70.

When Joan Littlewood staged *The Marie Lloyd Story* in the East London Theatre Royal in Stratford none of the cockney youngsters in the audience had ever heard any of the old music hall songs or indeed any real 'tunes' before. They were thrilled and startled. Then they returned to their transistors and Pepsi Cola.

Today the Pearlies begin to feel themselves more an anachronism than a tradition. For a generation their teenage children have usually

The newly elected Festival Pearly Queen of Britain, Mrs Beatrice Marriott, at the Festival of Britain celebrations in 1951.

preferred American dungarees to the glories of Pearly dress and found fashionable sponsored charity walks more to their liking than the old Pearly charity carnivals. But this climate is changing. There is today a national nostalgia for the old days and a real yearning for what is individual and English. For the first time since the early 1920s cockney girls are again wearing long skirts. Pease-pudding (which has never ceased to be sold in the little East End eating shops) is making a big come-back. And the youngsters are reported to be taking to beer. Is it too soon to hope for a rekindling of the authentic old cockney spirit?

Surely not! The famous Hoxton Nutley family, together with the Hitchens of Westminister and the City of London, staged a handsome Pearly crowning, on the retirement of Alf Meader, for their descendants in November 1974: Paul and Janet Groves (aged 17 and 14) became Pearly King and Queen of Hackney.

The enthusiasm of the Pearly youngsters is bound to be infectious and is a welcome augury. 'All we want to do now', says the new King Paul (a car mechanic), 'is to go out and start raising money'. The Reverent Austin Williams performed the crowning ceremony for this fifth generation of Pearly Royalty.

PROSPECT OF PEARLIES

Every Autumn on the first Sunday in October the London Pearlies never fail to make their way on foot, by bus, by taxi, and sometimes by car though never now by donkey-cart, to their annual Pearly Harvest Festival at the church of St Martins-in-the-Fields. Their friend the Reverend Austin Williams receives them wearing his pearl-buttoned black stole. The service is specially for them and each year a different Pearly King reads the lesson. 'It is a marvellous experience', says the minister, 'to hear the bible read in authentic cockney'.

Though their numbers diminish steadily each year the Pearlies still make a magnificent show, their flashing buttons and brilliant feathers lighting up the whole church. The Pearly Queens carry giant harvest loaves, and the little Pearly Princesses carry graceful baskets of vegetables. The church is decorated with homely cabbages, leeks, carrots and onions. It is a totally cockney occasion.

Every Pearly who can possibly make the journey is proud to take part, for it is one of their rare chances of assembling in force. There are aged Pearly Queen great-grandmothers with the regal bearing earned by a lifetime of sustaining the heavy Pearly dress; strong bodied, wiry Pearly coster Kings, their unmistakeably cockney-confident grins underlined by gay kingsmen and a gallant array of military medals pinned amongst the pearl buttons; handsome Pearly Queens glittering with jewels carefully chosen to match their Royal pearled dress; Pearly Princes proud in pearled waistcoats and bell-bottomed trousers, and little Pearly Princesses, solemn in their velvet frocks buttoned with small irridescent pearl buttons, their round faces excited under their feathered Edwardian bonnets. And here we must repeat, alas (though they looked more), at the 1973 Pearly Harvest Festival the total number of Pearlies was fourteen (eight of them belonging to the extensive Marriott family, including Beatrice Marriott's nephew Wiggy Marriott, Pearly King of Lambeth, who read the lesson. Wiggy who sums up the rôle of church service in family life: to match, hatch and dispatch).

Amongst the Pearlies present were the Pearly King and Queen of Peckham, George Major and his bright young wife, who brought their four pretty daughters; the son and heir she tried so hard to achieve, the infant Pearly Prince of Peckham, was still too young to make his appearance on this great occasion. The rest of the Pearlies had quarrelled or dropped out, were too infirm to attend or too young, or had already as the Pearlies say 'Gorn upstairs.' In 1974 there were also 14 Pearlies who attended the service. But, we must insist, there *are* hopeful signs of a Pearly renaissance. Not only are the young becoming enthusiastic, but the old Pearly feuds are beginning to heal – and just in time. The Pearlies feel, and how right they are, that England needs them today more than ever before.

But if the Pearlies have decreased in numbers they are certainly increasing in prestige. A century ago the Lord Mayor of London's 'blanket' (Banquet) meant to costers merely a date in the calender after which they could sell sprats. In 1973 not only were the Pearlies invited to take part in the Lord Mayor's Show, but Dowager Pearly Queen Mrs Beatrice Marriott and her daughter Marie-Louise were invited as special honoured guests to the Lord Mayor's Mansion House where Marie-Louise made a speech.

3.

LIVES
of the
PEARLIES

In 1960 Mrs Marguerite Fawdry, who was arranging an exhibition of Pearly dress and accessories for Pollock's Toy Museum, made a complete survey of all the then surviving Pearlies. With the help of the BBC she recorded on tape interviews with every Pearly Royal then alive, including Fred Tinsley, the Matthews, the Springfelds, the Turners, the Lodges, the Singfields, the Morrises, the Davidsons, the Montagues, the Emmings and the Marriotts. We cannot be sufficiently grateful to her for this historic effort as important and thorough in its day and timing as Mayhews' survey of the London costers of 1851.

Each Pearly Royal, in his or her own words, in rich and varied cockney accents, sometimes infused with a lingering Lancashire intonation, related his life history. To play back these tapes is to enter another world, the world of Cockney London in the early 1900s with its poverty, its toil and its hearty enjoyments, a much smaller London of gaslight, winkles, clammy pavements, raucous music hall songs and a passion for dressing up. It is from these tapes that the following biographies largely derive. A record of the London we have lost . . .

MR & MRS POMEROY (PEARLY KING & QUEEN OF KENTISH TOWN)

Mr Pomeroy's story is the classic Pearly story. A small wiry man, as so many London costers are, he managed to buy himself a donkey and cart and despite a lifetime of chronic asthma was earning a living for his family with a stall in the market. He joined the Pearlies and was elected Pearly King of Kentish Town. Despite his asthma he worked hard in his free time (Sundays and holidays) collecting for Pearly charities and took pleasure in designing and making his elaborate Pearly outfit; it was mushroom colour with a small check pattern, a bell coat with bell-bottomed trousers to match, both garments bordered with red velvet. The buttons were sewn on in a close but not smother pattern relieved by a scattering of 'red bugs'. His Pearly cap had a tassel of pearl beads and his jacket collar was outlined in orange-tinted buttons. Late in his life he was persuaded to sell this Pearly suit to someone in Australia. He immediately began to make himself a new Pearly outfit with modern plastic buttons (pearl ones being unobtainable) sewn in close patterns on to a brown melton suit made to measure.

He refused to sell his pearled whip.

An enthusiastic supporter of the famous donkey-shows, Mr Pomeroy won several rosettes for the 'Best turn-out' which he was proud to keep on show under a glass dome in his terrace house until the day came when his home was destroyed to make way for modern development. So Mr Pomeroy, like John Marriott, lost his donkey-stable, his donkey and his livelihood. He was rehoused and at the end of his life like so many other costers, and worked when he was well enough as a road-sweeper.

Mrs Pomeroy's Pearly outfit consisted of a navy-blue coat of serge, pearled shoes and a red velvet hat. Their two grandchildren's Pearly costumes were of blue velvet coats and hats trimmed with red, blue and white feathers. Trimmed with red buttons, the 'Three Pots a Shilling' motif of flowerpots was a favourite of the Pomeroy family, and Mr and Mrs Pomeroy, working together, made them all.

MR & MRS HALL (PEARLY KING & QUEEN OF WILLESDEN)

Mr Hall, a gentle small man who was deaf and almost blind in his old age, began his working life as a flower-seller in Kentish Town. He also made wreaths. He was always good with his hands and a meticulously neat and clean craftsman. He did not like tinted buttons or extravagant fancies. When he became a Pearly he only used the old type of button, thin flat English mother-of-pearl buttons, which he sewed onto his Pearly dress with white crochet cotton. He always drew his designs out on cardboard, then carefully chalked them onto the Pearly suit. Before going out to collect he always was careful to give the suit a good brushing and cleaned every individual button with Tide and a nailbrush. He also made Mrs Turner's Pearly outfit and those of his daughter and his grand-daughter. In his old age, when he could not keep on the flower-stall, he had to get a job in a factory sweeping floors. In his youth he served in the Royal Flying Corps in the First World War.

Mrs Hall, a good and careful housewife, quiet and gentle like her husband, followed him in all his undertakings, bringing up her family as Pearlies. Without his commitment she might never have become a Pearly herself, but since he was involved she involved herself too. She was in the ATS in the war.

MRS EMILY EMMINGS (PEARLY QUEEN OF BATTERSEA)

Emily Emmings was the widow of William James Emmings, Pearly King of Battersea. Daughter of a bricklayer, she was born, brought up, and lived all her life in Battersea. She was married in Battersea Old Church. Her husband went out on carnivals with his parents and won a 'Hospital collection 'medal at the age of twelve. He belonged to the 'Sons of Phoenix', a provident temperance society from which several Pearly Kings graduated. This society was organised into committees of twelve members who decided by voting how money should be raised and which charities to spend it on. At first they used to confine their efforts to tea-parties for deprived children, followed by entertainment. Later they worked for old people as well. Born the youngest of thirteen children, Emily Emmings was fifteen when she met her future husband, the son of a Thames lighterman, who had himself kept a street-stall. She worked in a local cake factory washing fruit. Then she went into the jam-making department which is where she met him. When he was old enough to be made a Pearly King he went out collecting officially for the Pearlies' charities, and he introduced long poles for collecting from people in top storeys. From the jam factory her husband went to work at Price's candle factory until he was called up in 1914. After the war he went to work for the Gas Company until he was pensioned off. A meticulous man, he kept every single receipt of his lifetime of collecting. He enjoyed every moment of his life of work, and his widow continued it after his death. Battersea was repeatedly bombed in the 1939 war, but Mrs Emmings stayed put (she had to have her windows replaced five times). Her proud moment came when old Queen Mary replied to her invitation and came to the street party she had organised for the local children to celebrate the victorious ending of World War Two, and to make up to them for the many nights underground during the bombings. She and her friends and their husbands washed and cleaned the whole street and decorated it handsomely (it took them three days), and set out trestle tables on both sides with a band to play in the middle. Clearly the old Queen took a fancy to Mrs Emmings and vice versa. She took a cup of tea with them, congratulated her on all the arrangements, and said it was the best of all the street-parties she had seen. 'Thank you Pearly Queen, that was lovely!', she said. After that they exchanged Christmas cards every Christmas. 'Queen Mary', said Mrs Emmings, 'was a dear old soul'. Mrs Emmings brought up her daughter's son and made his Pearly outfits for him, although at sixteen he lost interest in Pearlies. During their Pearly lives the Emmings collected many thousands of pounds.

MR & MRS GOLDEN (PEARLY KING & QUEEN OF WOOLWICH)

Mr Golden was born in Manchester and came to London at the age of fourteen. He served overseas during the 1914 war, ending as a sergeant in Rangoon (18th Rifle Brigade). He was football referee for the Burma Athletic Association. On his return to Woolwich he began joining the carnival in fancy dress, his favourite being a sailor in white ducks. He carried a metal lifeboat when he was collecting for lifeboat charities, and tried always to have an appropriate picture painted on his collection box according to the charity. He and his second wife Sarah (dressed as a miner and a nurse) collected money to help the miners' families after the Gresford mining disaster in North Wales.

Nearly all his life he was employed by the firm of W. T. Henley as a cable hand. He acquired his first Pearly suit (as Pearly 'helper') when a lodger in his house could not pay the rent and gave him his Pearly outfit in lieu. Later he was elected Pearly King of Woolwich and made himself a new Pearly outfit. Another lodger in his house made himself a Pearly outfit and gave himself the title of Pearly Prince of Woolwich.

William Golden was known amongst the Pearlies as the 'Royal' Pearly King because he had been presented on two different occasions to real Royalty, once to the then Prince of Wales (later Duke of

The silver medallion presented to Bill Golden,
Pearly King of Woolwich, by the Woolwich &
District War Memorial Hospital in 1946. Obverse
and reverse.

Windsor) and on another occasion to the then Duchess of Kent
(Princess Marina).

Mr Golden died in 1961 aged eighty. His last suit as Pearly King of
Woolwich was of dark grey chalk striped material (jacket) with 'All for
Charity' in buttons across the front. The trousers were black ornamented
with green, pink and blue pearl buttons. After his death the suit was
sent to New Zealand.

Mrs Sarah Ann Golden (his second wife), 81 years old in 1973, said
after her retirement, 'I have had a wonderful life and thank God for it.
I only hope and pray my eyesight will be kind to me so as I can carry
on making my dolls as it does bring so much happiness to the people
who receive them.' (They were of course Pearly dolls.) In a photograph
taken in his old age William Golden wore a pearled cap, pearled bow
tie, pearled walking stick, and pearl-button-bordered grey striped coat
which carried his war medals and rosettes, lucky horse-shoe, and 'Three
Pots a Shilling'; the black trousers are patterned with rayed suns,
cardinal pointed crosses and boots facing inwards. Mrs Golden's long
coat is made to match. She carried a pearled bag and is wearing a large
turned-back heavily feathered and pearled hat.

They had nine grandchildren and numerous great-grandchildren.

MR BERT LODGE (PEARLY KING OF THE BOROUGH)

Mr Lodge was a close friend of Mr and Mrs Montague and rented a room
in their house in Stonebridge Park. At one time a member of the Jolly-

boys Club (1919–1920) for whom he collected money dressed as a cowboy. He had no patience with the police who, he claimed, arrested him for 'shooting off his gun', this being his old army pistol, which was not loaded. He collected chiefly for hospitals.

In 1921 Bert Lodge joined the Pearlies and began to collect money for Guy's Hospital.

A Bermondsey-born Pearly, son of a bricklayer, Mr Lodge did all sorts of jobs to earn his living, such as store-keeping and motor-fitting. The job he liked best was machine-operating but this gave him dermatitis and he had to give it up.

He preferred to keep out of Pearly controversies and claimed to be without politics or religion in his charitable work. He was proud to have been appointed a life-Governor of London Hospital, after having worked for forty years 'in buttons'.

He liked the work of designing and sewing his Pearly outfit, and claimed credit for two innovations, sewing with red thread (which showed up well on the pearl buttons) and the substitution of a pearled collar and tie for the usual kingsman.

MR & MRS MONTAGUE (PEARLY KING & QUEEN OF STONE-BRIDGE PARK)

Mr Montague, a small neat man, a house-painter and decorator, was involved in the Pearly row over the blind girl which brought Mr Turner and Mr Hitchens into conflict. As a result of this Mr Montague preferred to conduct his Pearly work outside London so as to avoid further upsets with the other Pearlies. For instance, he and his wife used to take on engagements as far away from London as Coventry, despite the discomfort of long travel in their heavy Pearly dress.

Son of a part-time bricklayer, Mr Montague volunteered for the army at the age of fifteen in the Second World War, and became an officer in charge of a Civil Defence district in London during that war.

He was one of eight coster children and helped with the family barrow pushing past Golders Green Station. A friend of Tinsley,

Bert Lodge, Pearly King of the Borough, who was made a life Governor of the London Hospital after some 'forty years in butters'. The costume includes patterns of trefoil, hearts, diamonds, rosettes in squares, flowers, leaves, and smother borders. The decoration has even extended to the shoes.

Marriott and the Matthews, who fostered his interest in the Pearly work, he also claimed to have dismantled, as part of his Civil Defence work, a 55lb shell bomb. He attended the Coventry Carnivals for fifteen years, and brought up his children to be Pearlies too.

He personally knew the misery of the London poor and was always against the police and felt it right to bait them. In one of his jobs, as bookmaker's runner, he was taken up for 'loitering and begging' but as his rent book was in arrears he escaped a fine.

He recalled buying 'sold-off' food at the end of the day from Whiteley's store when you could pick up a chicken not in its first freshness for one shilling or one shilling and sixpence. He and his brothers and sisters used to buy a pillow-slip full of stale bread (from the previous day) for threepence. His mother made bread puddings out of these left-overs.

Mr Montague preferred a pearled collar-and-tie to a kingsman, and made use, as his Pearly dress motif, of a design he copied from the glass-door of a public house. He had one daughter, Pamela, and a son, Ron.

Mrs Montague worked in a factory as a girl. By the time she became a Pearly Queen the price of pearl buttons had risen from one shilling or one shilling and sixpence a gross (English water-pearl) to eighteen shillings a gross and even at that price they had become practically unobtainable. Her husband auctioned his Pearly dress to raise funds for crippled children. Her son Ron was the youngest Pearly King in London (Kensington).

MR & MRS MEADER (PEARLY KING & QUEEN OF HACKNEY)

By all accounts Alfred Meader was a supremely happy self-confident man, who threw himself into everything he did, doing it well and with zest. Son of an engineer, Mr Meader joined the army at fifteen and a half and fought in both world wars. He played the banjo and had a powerful singing voice, playing at many semi-professional concerts and professional music halls. He worked as a piano-tuner. He sang at the Britannia in Hoxton as a child of nine with Marie Kendall, for which his father was paid one guinea a week. He also sang in the church choir. Later, after he had organised and collected money for many outings for poor children, he was elected Pearly King of Hackney.

He became a senior messenger for the Civil Service for whom he worked for very many years. With seven children of his own, all of whom grew up and duly married and had children of their own, he was particularly interested in the organisation of children's outings and the

Fund for Blind Babies, and he also worked for the British Legion. At one time he organised an outing of one thousand children to Southend. There was no trouble at all, he said, and not a child missing at any stage. It was, he claimed, entirely a matter of good organisation, the right stewards and helpers, and co-operation with the children concerned. He had a bet on the success of this outing, which he won.

Into old age Mr Meader was out almost every night and all weekends collecting for his favourite charities. He made his own Pearly dress and helped Mrs Meader with hers. Mr Meader chose the three-feather symbol of the Prince of Wales for his Pearly motif which he worked out in large pearl buttons on the back of his Pearly jacket. He also introduced touches of gold paint into some of the accompanying buttons. With each button knotted on separately the outfit took him seven and a half months to complete.

He was careful to keep out of any Pearly feuds. As an old man he could still give a powerful rendering of 'Girl of My Dreams' accompanying himself on the banjo.

Mrs Meader's Pearly Queen outfit was distinguished by the introduction of bugle beads in red, white and green, sewed on to the skirt in triangles. In order to have the pleasure of his company as much as to help his favourite charities, Mrs Meader used to put on her Pearly costume at weekends and go out collecting with him, although she must have been tired after her week's work in a canteen and looking after her large family. On the retirement of Mr Meader, Janet and Paul Groves were crowned the new King and Queen of Hackney (see above).

MR & MRS TURNER (PEARLY KING & QUEEN OF EDMONTON)

Mr Turner's life was taken up with the care of animals, with a desperate struggle to earn his living which brought him close to the daily problems of the needy and so into the Pearly movement, and with his horrible experience as a soldier in the First World War.

He was born in Manchester, joined the army in 1914 and at the age of twenty-one was blinded in a gas attack (Ypres, 1916). He returned to England, attended hospital for nearly a year and never afterwards could forget the wards packed with badly wounded soldiers. When he recovered his eyesight he was sent back to the front where he fought till the end of the war.

He had no war pension. In 1919 he slowly made his way to London looking for work. He joined a travelling fair as handyman, and devoted himself to the horses. It was a period of massive unemployment and the condition of the children he encountered on his travels distressed him so much that he started helping in his own way. He used to go round with a big sack collecting old boots so that the children should not go barefoot in the winter, and he started dressing-up and singing at charity concerts and carnivals, at one of which, dressed as Dick Turpin, he won two awards and met Kate Carney whom the Pearlies regarded as their Goddess. He got to know Henry Croft and eventually became a Pearly himself.

By now he was earning a modest living as a carrier with two ponies to care for. After his first wife died he married again. He had five children, losing two daughters very young. A good Catholic, Mr Turner was also a member of the 'Old Contemptibles' and punctilious in his attendance at their yearly service in St Paul's Cathedral.

He was inclined to act as a Pearly on his own for individual needy cases, and this is contrary to Pearly policy, lest it lead to dislocation of effort and even trouble with authority. The affair of the blind girl he collected for (in perfectly good faith) to send her to a special school for the blind in Scotland turned out disastrously. There was not enough money collected to keep her on at the school and then it was discovered that the girl's father was a well-to-do publican who could have paid the fees himself. This caused a Pearly row in which Mr Turner felt himself unjustly treated, especially by Fred Hitchens who was the initial mover in the effort and to whom Mr Turner would not speak afterwards. He was a great admirer of Henry Croft and regarded himself as a pioneer.

Still keeping house when well over eighty, the second Mrs Turner, like Mr Turner, was devoted to animals and anything needing care. They lived in the same little house in Edmonton for over fifty years, in a neat black and white terrace. They kept coronation mugs on their dresser and were proud of their old copper warming pan and old hanging clock. Like other Pearlies they based their way of life on traditional rituals and objects. Even after thirty years' effort they could never get used to their false teeth and only put them in when visitors called at their cottage. They kept a dog and several cats which were

Mrs Turner, the Pearly Queen of Edmonton, at home in 1960. She was one of the first generation Pearlies and her patterned dress, decorated with scattered rosettes augmented with brooches, is cut in the style of the 1910-14 period.

fed with cow's milk, though the Turners used tinned milk for them-selves. They were very hospitable and loved to give a big high tea to whoever called, though they themselves hardly ate anything. They also had the care of an invalid son-in-law whose limbs had been crushed in an accident. Of their five grandchildren, all brought up to be Pearlies, Mrs Turner had the highest hopes for Mary Armitage, to whom she resigned her Pearly Queen crown when she abdicated the Pearly throne of Edmonton at the age of eighty-four.

MR & MRS SINGFIELD (PEARLY KING & QUEEN OF WHITE-CHAPEL, LATER OF DAGENHAM)

The Singfields were a widespread lively family, one of the great Pearly dynasties which the two world wars have so cruelly shattered. A real cockney character, this Mr Singfield was practically born on the stage in the East End of London, being used as a stage prop at the age of five weeks, his mother hiring him out at three shillings and sixpence an hour. Both his parents were music hall artists and he spent much of his child-hood in the music halls. But as he grew older he fancied himself more as a coster. He ran stalls in Petticoat Lane and several other markets, enjoying the spieling. And buying and selling anything that turned up, boots, toys, haberdashery, whatever he could buy cheaply enough. He had a pony and cart. He was an early member of the Labour Party (unlike most costers who tend to keep off politics). His evenings Mr Singfield devoted to concerts and political processions, having a talent for organising. When he became a Pearly he made himself a splendid outfit, 'smother' style with pearled accessories: walking-stick, gloves, wallet, cigarette case and match box all smothered in pearl buttons. It must have been extraordinarily heavy. But then he had his own transport. He was devoted to his pony and cart which he decorated lavishly.

During the 1914 war he served with the Royal Flying Corps and per-formed with concert parties entertaining the troops. He lost his airman son, shot down in the 1939 war. In his memory he has created a garden of statuettes and flowers in his small Dagenham home, where he lived in retirement, working in a factory which he disliked. Mr Springfield was the link between the early Labour banner-marches and the Pearly carnivals. Certainly he remembered that the Labour marchers used to give whatever they had to the Pearly collecting boxes.

Mrs Singfield, as a girl, worked in a button factory. After the birth of her children she stayed home to look after them. A good wife and mother she supported her husband in all his enterprises including his Pearly activities.

MR & MRS MORRIS (PEARLY KING & QUEEN OF BETHNAL GREEN)

Mrs Morris came from Sheffield, but has become so assimilated by Cockney London that it is impossible to know she was not born within the sound of Bow Bells. Mr Morris worked in Smithfield Meat Market. During the war Mrs Morris worked on munitions. They were both keen helpers in the carnivals, collecting for London hospitals. Always large and plump, Mrs Morris was able to wear her Pearly outfit for forty years, almost a record. Ever since joining the Pearlies (in the 1920s) Mrs Morris has been a very close friend of Mrs Beatrice Marriott, and they are usually seen together in the old photographs. Mrs Morris was a Londoner by residence for fifty-two years.

MR & MRS HARRY SPRINGFIELD (PEARLY KING & QUEEN OF STOKE NEWINGTON)

The Springfields are related to the Marriotts. Rosie Springfield, widow of the late Harry Springfield, being Beatrice Marriott's niece. Like his father, who was a Pearly coster in Leather Lane Market, Holborn, Harry Springfield was also a coster all his life, though he managed later to acquire a motor van. One aspect of the coster life however remained unchanged for over a century. Like costers in Mayhew's time, Harry Springfield always rose at 4 a.m., just as they did, all his life to get to Smithfield Market to lay out his stockmoney in good time.

Harry Springfield made his own Pearly dress, worked out his own designs and did everything himself. He fancied coloured pearl and used to dye his buttons with Drummer dyes. He was active at weekends, collecting for the needy in his Pearly dress.

He did up their little terrace house in Edmonton himself.

He was a big dark man.

Rosie Springfield (they have five children) worked in a factory before her marriage (she herself was one of fifteen children). A slim young-looking grandmother at fifty, she inherited the Marriott energy and self-

Ageing Pearly Royalty: Bill and Martha Morris, the Pearly King and Queen of Bethnal Green, collecting in Piccadilly Circus in 1958.

Mrs Rosie Springfield, the Pearly Queen of Stoke
Newington, in 1960. Her regalia is supplemented by
elaborate pearl chandelier ear-rings, pearl necklaces,
diamenté ornaments on the hat, and many brooches.

confidence. Quick-witted, she appeared on TV and won a handsome set of kitchen furniture in pale blue and white which started them off redecorating their little house, though it was only rented. Their sons are now married and one has a child of his own, a daughter who was christened in the famous Marriott family christening Pearly robe worn by four generations.

Unlike some of the other Pearly Princes and Princesses, especially in their teens, the Springfield children have all enjoyed wearing Pearly dress and take an active interest in Pearly activities, though the Springfield boys were also devoted to their black leather studded teenage outfits at the same time.

The entire Springfield family wore Pearly dress, and as the children arrived new ones were made for them, the fourth generation of Springfield Pearlies.

Rosie Springfield is noted for the panache of her Pearly dress, the size and multitude of feathers trimming it, and the brilliance of the jewels adorning it. She wears many rows of pearl necklaces with her Pearly outfit and huge chandelier pearl earrings.

MR EDWARD 'WIGGY' MARRIOTT (PEARLY KING OF LAMBETH)

Edward Marriott is a nephew of Beatrice Marriott, and an entertainer and charity-collector in the old tradition.* He worked in Covent Garden as a lorry driver and drove tanks in the 1939 war. He was a fitter in the Royal Tank Corps. In Islington when he was a youth they used to hold contests of caged linnets, chaffinches or bullfinches, and collected bets on which could sing loudest and longest, to raise money to help the local sick and the unemployed. 'The smaller the cage the better they sing.'

His elder brother had a stall in the local market and a horse and cart, and they also pushed a barrow on Sunday mornings. Even so it was hard work to earn enough then to provide that essential Sunday dinner.

Edward Marriott (nicknamed Wiggy) started wearing pearlies when a child. He specialised in collecting for poor children's outings. Islington Pearlies (largely the Marriott family) on one occasion organised such an outing for 2000 children from Islington who were taken to Barnet in horse-brakes.

Today a short stocky man, strongly built like all the Marriotts, he delights in his cockney background, and he drives a sightseeing coach

*Orphaned young he was brought up in the family of his aunt, Beatrice Marriott. And in later life himself brought up several orphans.

Two old-style Pearly Kings: Wiggy Marriott, the
nephew of Beatrice Marriott, with Mr Major,
Pearly King of Peckham.
Wiggy, Pearly King of Lambeth, is wearing an
historic regalia jacket with smother pattern front
and war medals. His pearly cap is edged with three
pearl necklaces.
Mr Major's regalia jacket and cap are embroidered
in horizontal lines, rosettes, and repeat smother
triangles.

for a big London firm. This gives him an ideal opportunity to use his wit and skill in entertainment. He is a marvellous pub pianist. He feels that the Pearlies have become little more than a tourist attraction.

Mrs Edward Marriott (Pearly Queen of Lambeth) is a quiet person devoted to her home (a terraced house they have done up themselves in contemporary style), her husband and their two children, a boy and a girl now adult, and neither keen on keeping up the Pearly tradition though both have Pearly outfits. Their two grandchildren, however, accompanied Wiggy Marriott to the 1973 Harvest Festival Service at the church of St Martins-in-the-Fields, both in Pearly dress.

MR BERT MATTHEWS (PEARLY KING OF HAMPSTEAD)

Bert Matthews was a small dark man with a high colour. As a boy he worked for a butcher, then for a fishmonger. West End customers then, he said, were waited on like royalty. They thought nothing of ordering one small fillet of plaice which Matthews had to trek the length of London in all sorts of weather to deliver. After he was married and had a family there were times when he tried to make ends meet by chopping and selling firewood. His family lived on 'penny pieces' (the old 'block ends' of Mayhew's day) which, with a pennyworth of pot-herbs, Mrs Matthews, who was always an excellent housewife and manager, made into nourishing stews.

Work was hard to get, and to earn a shilling or one shilling and sixpence, counted as a good day. Bert Matthews always longed for a small shop of his own. This he never achieved. For years he was rat-catcher for the Hampstead Borough – 'I think I gave them a clear up!'. In those days, early in the twentieth century, foxes and badgers lurked in the Hampstead woods, sheep and cattle grazed on Golders Green, and in the summer, there was hay-making on Hampstead Heath.

Although his little shop eluded him he did become a coster and finally ran a whelk stall on Sunday mornings in Hampstead which also sold cockles and hot potatoes. This was kept going into the 1960s.

He and Mrs Matthews were enthusiastic and very early Pearlies, and also delighted in music halls. His first Pearly suit was on checked material. Mrs Matthews sewed the buttons and decided and arranged the designs in consultation with her husband.

When they were able to afford a donkey, and finally a pony, they attended all the donkey-shows and won many prizes. He had a glass case filled with the rosettes they won for the 'best turn-out'.

133

The Matthews were chosen to represent the London Pearlies at the Coronation of Queen Elizabeth the Second for which they both made new Pearly outfits. Mr Matthews wore a 'massed' button suit with an elegant coster waistcoat sporting six pockets and a small collar. For the Coronation Mrs Matthews designed and made her Pearly dress and coat of pale blue velvet decorated with trails of flowers with red and blue centres.

Later in life, by this time a famous Pearly King, Mr Matthews (with Mrs Matthews) accompanied Trade Fairs to the USA, Canada and Holland. A BBC feature programme was built round them. In America their Pearly costumes were displayed in Macey's. Their daughter Rose (taking the name Matthews-Smith when she married) became the controversial Pearly Queen of Hampstead, and her husband, George, the disputed King, became Prince Consort on the death of Bert Matthews, then aged over eighty-five.

MRS REBECCA MATTHEWS (PEARLY QUEEN OF HAMPSTEAD)

One of the earliest Pearly photographs ever taken shows Mrs Matthews in her coster dress in the 1890s, a good-looking young woman wearing a lightly pearled jacket with leg-of-mutton sleeves, a large feathered hat, and tulip-shaped skirt over which she is wearing a traditional coster girl's long starched white apron with a flounced frill round the hem. In 1902 there is another photograph of her in different Pearly dress without the apron, and her forward-tilted feathered hat shows the change of fashion as also does the different cut of the jacket. That year she and her husband began collecting for the hospital on Hampstead Heath. She was always an enthusiastic able worker for the Pearlies and one of those women who do everything well they undertake. She had a strong artistic talent and planned and made their Pearly dresses with great skill. 'She can do anything', her family said of her. Whilst Mr Matthews was delivering newspapers at 5 a.m. she had been working in a local laundry, a thirteen hour day – 8 a.m. to 9 p.m. The work included callendering and goffering and changing the heavy

Bert Matthews, the Pearly King of Hampstead, in 1960.
This back view of his regalia coat shows the six-pointed star, rosettes, crown, horse shoe and horse's head, rainbows, smother filling-in, eyes of God and Union Jack patterns.

irons. Piecework rates meant earning two-pence for a servant's long print dress (ironing, starching and folding) and a half penny for a servant's muslin apron, goffering included. The laundresses sang all the time, music hall songs mostly. To earn a bare wage you had to work very fast. But they were a close happy family. 'Everyone used to help each other', her daughter said.

She always drove with her husband to the great donkey-shows. In those days it took them seven hours to drive to the Derby. Mrs Matthews had several fine Pearly dresses for she looked after them so carefully that they lasted over fifty years. Her Pearly outfits included an apricot-coloured coat and a crimson silk hat with ostrich feathers.

MR & MRS PINAUD (PEARLY KING & QUEEN OF GREENWICH & WOOLWICH)

Though many Pearly Royals were born outside London, George Pinaud was perhaps the only Pearly King who was a foreigner. It was difficult to keep the royalty restricted to those born in London and impossible to confine them to those born within the sound of Bow Bells (especially as the important South London Pearlies could not fall within that category). By the time he became a Pearly King the old regulations were lapsing, and in fact he was not asked to take on the office but applied for it.

George Pinaud was born in Jersey in the Channel Islands. As a young man he kept a stall in Greenwich Market. Despite the fact that he had only one lung he was an enthusiastic amateur music hall performer, his speciality being a drag act. Later in life he worked for the Gas Board. A devout Catholic, he was a working member of the local Greenwich Catholic Club. He was an able craftsman who enjoyed painting elaborate glass pictures and designed and made his own costume. He and his wife Kitty (the only non-British Pearly Queen) obviously enjoyed ceremonial dressing-up.

When they discovered that there was no extant Pearly King and Queen of Greenwich the Pinauds applied to the Town Clerk of Greenwich 'for the post'. This is a most irregular proceeding and shows how far away from its origins the office had drifted. They were allotted the 'post' which was of course honorary but involved many public appearances in borough functions. They collected money for charity too, but they made, it appears, more of the ceremonial side.

Mrs Pinaud did not approve of the ebullient coster Pearly image of

'Polly is the winner!' Mr and Mrs Bert Matthews, the Pearly King and Queen of Hampstead, lead their donkey and cart in to receive the prize at the Regents Park Donkey and Pony Show in 1934.

137

tradition with its bright silk kingsman and buttoned cap, so she persuaded her husband to have a top hat and bow tie covered with buttons as 'less vulgar'. On being accorded the royal office, the Pinauds made themselves elaborate stage Pearly crowns, and they were thus crowned in 1958. Mrs Pinaud, it seems, was the partner pushing in the direction of gentility. She always wore white gloves (long ones in the evening) and had made a special Pearly evening cape, seed-pearl evening bag, etc.

George Pinaud made himself several elaborate Pearly outfits. He liked coloured buttons and tinted them himself with Tintex. He made his own patterns, rich and set close and very neatly sewn. He also designed and made all his wife's many Pearly garments.

George Pinaud was a small man with a little moustache and spectacles, and perhaps was better remembered after his death as a former 'drag act' amateur entertainer than as a Pearly King.

Mrs Kitty Pinaud who for years kept a dress-stall in Greenwich Market, is a good-looking Irish woman, slim and volatile, with clear interests in display and elegance. She has not, nor would ever wish to have, the old heartiness and common touch of the early Pearly Royalties.

After her husband's death she decided to sell his Pearly outfit (for £500) and wished either Greenwich or some other London borough to buy it. If this should fall through she proposed to sell the outfit to an American museum.

MRS BEATRICE MARRIOTT (CITY OF LONDON FESTIVAL PEARLY QUEEN)

Mrs Beatrice Marriott (whose father-in-law, John Marriott, was the first Pearly King of Finsbury) is one of the few surviving Pearlies from the early days. A big handsome old lady, cheerful and bubbling with cockney wit, she presides over her children and grandchildren and great-grandchildren from her neat council flat in North London. She collects and dyes ostrich feathers to adorn Pearly Queen hats ('got a friend in the trade') and tints precious pearl buttons. Still very active, it was she

The back view of the regalia jacket of George Pinaud, Pearly King of Greenwich and Deptford. The patterns include title, smother, rosettes, and demi–lunes.
1971.

Mrs Beatrice Marriott, the Festival Pearly Queen of London, teaches the Italian dockers the 'Lambeth Walk' and enlivens the launching ceremony of the P. & O. cruiser *Spirit of London* at Genoa in 1972.

who was chosen to launch the new P. & O. cruising ship *Spirit of London* from Genoa. Although she had never been to Europe before, she flew there, broke the bottle of champagne on the bows of the new vessel and made her speech with splendid calm and dignity.

The Earl of Inchcape of the P. & O. Shipping Lines writes of this occasion – 'Our first – and memorable – encounter with Mrs Marriott was in 1972 at Genoa when she launched our new cruise ship, *Spirit of London*, with all the panache of a veteran sponsor. She was also an immediate success with the Italian shipyard workers who were captivated by her attempts to teach them the Lambeth Walk.' (*Spirit of London* is now based on the west coast of America where she is making a valuable contribution to Britain's overseas invisible earnings.)

Something of the old tough gaiety of early days is still with Mrs Marriott. She is a woman of decision and steadfastness in emergency.

When her son John died in 1971 (he had been Pearly King of Finsbury and leader of all the London Pearly activities – taking over on the death of her husband who had died in 1954) it was Mrs Beatrice Marriott who held the distressed family and all the London Pearlies together, keeping on the Pearly work and making the intricate Pearly collecting and organising arrangements from her council flat.

Beatrice Marriott had a tough happy childhood in a large coster family. She remembers pushing their kitten in a doll's pram covered with a lace curtain all the way to Regent's Park for a picnic in the school holidays, together with her brothers and sisters, with a picnic-bag of broken biscuits and a bottle of water. Such long walks were thought nothing of. Every Friday night all the family were taken by their parents to the local music hall with a large bag of boiled sweets for their weekly treat. She learned all the popular songs this way from hearing them sung by the best music hall stars.

In her teens, she and John (who wanted to marry) took on all sorts of jobs to earn money to save up for a donkey of their own. At one time she worked in a factory making artificial flowers. It was her husband, John, who founded the Pearly Kings & Queens Association in 1910. She has lived through tragedy, seen her husband die young at 55, and her son John (who took over his Pearly outfit and responsibilities most ably) also die young, and now the fourth Pearly King of Finsbury, *his* son John, a boy still in his teens, and far from robust, take on the Kingship and try to assume the extremely heavy mass-pearled royal outfit.

So far the Marriotts have had more than twenty Pearly Kings and Queens in their family history. She has always cherished the memory of Princess Marie-Louise who was a friend and who presented a special Royal Armlet of red velvet and gold to them, in appreciation of their work for charity, after the 1927 Pearly Ball her husband arranged. One of her daughters, now Pearly Queen of Finsbury, is named Marie-Louise after the Princess who was her godmother.

Beatrice Marriott has made and worn many Pearly outfits in the course of her long life. The one she wears today is probably the heaviest of any worn by any Pearly. It has a totally mass-pearled 'smother' long coat and skirt containing in all something like 90,000 pearl buttons. It is of dark cloth which cannot be seen beneath the buttons. Her cartwheel hat is bordered by pearl buttons and adorned with a sparkling round brooch on the inside brim and sixteen large ostrich plumes (red,

Mrs Beatrice Marriott, the Festival Pearly Queen of London, at the party in the crypt of St Martins-in-the-Fields after the Harvest Festival Service in 1973. Notice particularly her smother patterned regalia coat, her sun-ray pattern handbag, and the jewelled hat with red, white and blue ostrich feathers.

white and blue, and one bright yellow). Mrs Marriott curls these herself regularly with a blunt knife. She also has a handsome long lavender velvet pearled coat.

Her grand-daughter Jean, a big fresh-complexioned witty young woman, remembers Mrs Marriott taking her out collecting in her Pearly dress when she was a little girl to learn the job. They are devoted to one another and Jean (although she married an Irishman, John O'Shea,

As he said, Pearly children were 'Bred and born in Pearlies and don't know no different'.

In 1959 the stables where he kept his pony were pulled down and he was out of a job. (The missionary ladies who had forced the stables on them a century earlier thus had unwittingly prepared the way for their subsequent ruin when these stables should no longer be allowed to occupy space the developers wanted for high-rise offices.)

This was a bitter blow to John Marriott and all the other costers who also lost their stables. He learned electronics which he was good at, and so was able to make a decent living for his family, but the work bored him. He missed his outdoor life as a coster, though it was physically much harder work than electronics. He missed the different patterns of the days and the backchat with his customers. He said he did not feel like a human being any more.

He and his wife Rose lived in a pleasant council flat in Islington. He enjoyed *Till Death Do Us Part* on TV and considered Alf Garnett very true to life as a Wapping cockney character.

He died suddenly in 1971. There was a great Pearly funeral widely reported in the Press.

MR AND MRS FRED TINSLEY (PEARLY KING & QUEEN OF SOUTHWARK)

Tinsley was born in 1890. He was a tall, thin, intelligent man. His father was originally a cotton-spinner who, thrown out of employment, learned to make and sell dulcimers at thirty shillings each, being very musical and able to play a variety of instruments. He sometimes did a turn at local music halls, especially the Old Canterbury, but also did street turns. Fred Tinsley himself could play the piano and the mouth organ and was taught clog-dancing as a boy by his father, many of whose family were dancers. These clogs, which Billingsgate porters still wear, are common wear of Lancashire weavers. Tinsley's father came south from Lancashire, to find employment.

When very young Fred Tinsley sold watercress and lettuce from a stall in the London street markets. His first efforts for charity were with

The Pearlies today: John Marriott the 4th wearing his grandfather's Festival Pearly regalia with his girl friend, Pat Gamble, wearing his sister Linda's regalia dress.
1971.

147

the Jollyboys Club. It was Henry Croft who inspired him to join the Pearlies after he had reached the distinction of becoming secretary to the Jollyboys Club where he first collected in a clown disguise. He was admitted into the Pearlies in 1911. He entertained his audiences with clog-dancing (wearing special wooden-soled clogs with wooden heels and metal tips) and singing popular songs such as 'My Old Man's a Fireman' and,

> 'Tike me for a walk all rahnd the 'ahses
> Take me to the opra or the ply . . . '

His first Pearly dress was a 'skeleton' style (that is, the pearl buttons outlining lapels, pockets and hems) which he copied from Albert Chevalier who had copied it from a genuine coster dress with its early Pearly design. To this basic pattern Tinsley continued to add pearl buttons. He bought his pearl buttons from Gardeners' Corner (the famous sailors' uniforms and livery outfitters in Whitechapel, now pulled down) at a cost of 4½d or 2½d per gross, according to size. He had an accurate eye for measurement and proportion and sewed on his buttons without chalk marks to guide him. He preferred using different coloured threads. The crown design on the back of his Pearly dress was taken from an ornamental crown he once saw in the window of Edgington's (the tent-makers of the Old Kent Road). He was a patient and persevering man. Sewing his Pearly outfit he once sat up all night for eleven hours at a stretch. He also sewed his wife's Pearly Queen outfit for her. His first Pearly suits were made of checked or dark material and he tried to get smoked buttons for them like Albert Chevalier's.

He was a great believer in experience, both in making Pearly dress and in the system of Pearly collection. 'As we go along so we improve all the time.'

He was a coster till 1914, selling his lettuces at two or three for a penny, and cucumbers at one and a half pence a piece. He lived most of his life in a very small house off the Old Kent Road.

It was Fred Tinsley who set up the original Pearly Guild. He fought in the 1914 war, was wounded at Chambroi, sent back to England and given a small pension. After that he became a chimney-sweep, and continued in this job until his retirement. It was sweeping the chimneys of old age pensioners (some were over ninety) that gave him the idea

Mr and Mrs Fred Tinsley, the Pearly King and Queen
of Southwark, with their grandson in 1960.

of organising an Old Age Pensioners' Outing. He had found them in such economic difficulties that he either swept their chimneys half-price or more often swept them for nothing.

He organised outings, such as a day at the seaside for two coachloads of OAPs each year. He collected money for and organised a New Year Party for one hundred old people each year too. Amongst his other charities were the Sunshine Homes for Blind Babies and Guy's Hospital. (In the miners' strike of 1926 Pearlies collected money to feed their families, selling replicas of miners' lamps to help the funds.) He was ingenious in his methods. At the Elephant and Castle he persuaded drinkers to put all their small change into his collecting box.

In his lifetime he worked for sixty-one years for charity. He told an interviewer in 1960: 'You've got to come out and help', and added, 'We had to make our own enjoyments. I don't envy young people in any way. They don't stop to think.'

He had two sons. The elder was killed in the Second World War.

Mrs Tinsley came from a large cockney family. Her father and mother were both street entertainers as were her uncles. Clog-dancing on a slate was the family speciality, accompanied by the harmonium played by an uncle. As a girl she sold oranges outside the old Surrey Theatre. She wore a white blouse, black shawl and black skirt ornamented with buttons at hem and sides. She collected money for the Surgical Aid Society and for the repair of Bow Bells. She lived all her long married life in the same little house off the Old Kent Road. Fred had a telephone installed finally for his charity organising but Mrs Tinsley did not take to telephones and never used it. She lived to be over seventy-nine.

MR BILL DAVIDSON (PEARLY KING OF WEST HAM, NOW NEWHAM) & MRS BILL DAVIDSON

Bill Davidson was a docker all his life, except when he was with the army in both world wars. A very tall, gaunt man, he is the poorest of all the Pearly Royalty and his regalia is the most beautifully made, strong in designs of triangles filled with exquisitely tinted small pearl identical buttons. He makes all his own Pearly outfits (sewn on to slop-shop dress), also his wife's Pearly dress and the cap and jacket of Rover,

Mr and Mrs Bill Davidson, the Pearly King and Queen of Newham (formerly West Ham), on the balcony of their Canning Town council flat in 1972. At their feet sits their dog Rover.

his Pearly dog whom he has taught to bark 'thank you' for contributions. He enjoyed the carnivals.

He can no longer work in the docks, being in his seventies, and he is on relief. He lives in a cold little council flat overlooking the Thames with his dog Rover and mementoes of his life and work. He joined the Royal Engineers in World War Two and fought at Tobruk. Though he cannot afford to warm his little flat properly, and he had the care and responsibility of his wife, he still goes out collecting in his pearlies. He told me there is no pleasure in life like collecting a lot of money, when you have none yourself, and then giving it all away to those still worse off than you are. Often he joins a carnival as far away as Southend. When they need a Pearly they let him know and he turns up with Rover and his collecting box.

A true old Pearly still, he has no high opinion of the police (a view which many costers and dockers still hold). Nevertheless he has appeared and done a turn at a policemen's charity concert.

Like other Pearlies of his age he seems to belong to the world of Charles Dickens and his speech is nearer Sam Weller's than today's speech. He refers to his kingsman as his 'stook' (which is the 18th century pronunciation of 'stock') or kerchief or cravat. The East End retains its ancient habits and expressions far longer than the West End. Even today the older dockers still wear knotted white silk scarves round their necks (without tie or collar) like the 18th century classic cravats.

Mrs Davidson started her working life as a domestic servant in her young teenage. Then she progressed to being a servant in the hospital and then became cook in the hospital. She had always wanted to be a Pearly and after she married Bill, 'I got my wish'. She was in delicate health in her old age and Bill looked after her. She was proud of the

The total Pearly way of life! Rover was one of a succession of dogs who went on carnivals collecting with Bill Davidson, the Pearly King of West Ham. Bill made Rover his own Pearly cap and Pearly jacket which were inscribed with 'All for Charity'. Rover also had a pipe and spectacles of his own and was trained to bark a 'thank you' for donations put into his collecting box. Rover was eventually given a medal by the many hospitals he collected for.
1960.

The tomb at Finchley cemetery of Henry Croft and his family, with a monument of him in his famous Pearly dress.
Henry Croft was the first Pearly King of Somerstown and the original and founder of all the Pearlies.
1930.

fact that Rover had won a medal for his charity collecting. She died in the early 1970s.

MR HENRY CROFT (PEARLY KING OF SOMERSTOWN)

Henry Croft, to whom all Pearlies look as their founder, was not a coster and unlike most costers he neither drank nor smoked. He was just about five feet high. He was a municipal road-sweeper all his life for St Pancras Borough Council. He had a very large family including one son who was killed in the 1914 war, and a daughter who helped him in his charitable work (which according to tradition Mrs Croft resented) and a grand-daughter who died at the age of five. None of his children continued his Pearly charity work after his death.

According to Ted ('Wiggy') Marriott (Pearly King of Lambeth), Henry Croft was first inspired to take up charity collecting by his two coster friends who always devoted a portion of their earnings from their stall to charity. Croft is believed to have taken the idea of his totally pearl button covered dress from a local music hall entertainer of the time who wore a stage costume entirely covered with brass buttons.

Though he died as he had lived all his life, a poor man, Henry Croft in his lifetime collected, in half pennies, pennies and farthings, over £5000 for charity. (This in today's values would amount to £200,000.)

His funeral in 1930 was a spectacular Pearly occasion with banners and bagpipes, and was filmed by Pathé News. No less than 400 Pearlies (all those then alive) carrying banners and leading their donkeys and ponies followed his coffin to the Finchley cemetery where he was buried.

A memorial statue (sculpted and carved in Tottenham) shows Henry Croft in his famous buttoned costume.

Appendix

'*THREE POTS*
A SHILLING'

KATE CARNEY *was born in 1870, she lived to be 80 and was singing to enraptured audiences almost to the end. Her rich throbbing contralto voice and her extrovert personality were ideally suited to the cockney coster songs she made her own. Of these the most famous and the most loved is still 'Three Pots a Shilling', known also as 'When the Summer comes again'. This song is still a favourite with old women in Canning Town and Plaistow, some of whom, when girls in their teens, sang it with Kate Carney herself on stage in the old East End music halls.*

In its pre-occupation with the vagaries of the weather, the temper of the moke, and its dream of fine clothes, it is pure coster, perhaps the nearest to a genuine love-song the costers could accept.

The Pearlies have taken over this song along with Kate Carney as their own, and many Pearlies have worked the motif of 'Three Pots a Shilling' on their jackets and waistcoats, and even on their trousers and skirts.

157

When The Summer Comes Again

Sung by MISS KATE CARNEY

Tune Ukulele

G C E A

Written and Composed by
HARRY BEDFORD
Arr. by Dudley E. Bayford

1. Oh! won't we have some mon-.ey, Nell, When the sum-mer comes a-
2. Sweet win-dow flow'rs then you'll cry, Nell, When the sum-mer comes a-
3. Oh! won't we turn out dash-ing, Nell, When the sum-mer comes a-

-gain, Life will be all hon-ey, gell,
-gain, Toffs from us will buy 'em, gell,
-gain, Folks will talk a-bout it, gell,

F. & D. Ltd. 2295

When the sum-mer comes a-gain; We shall roam all round the
When the sum-mer comes a-gain; For I knows the best of
When the sum-mer comes a-gain; You shall dress in 'brosh-ey'

E7   Am   C7

coun-try With pret-ty flow'rs, sun-shine or rain, Straight! we'll
hous-es, Where lots of pro-fit we can gain, Splen-did
vel-vet, me a sil-ver watch and chain, Let coves

F   C7   F

buy up Cov-ent Gar-den, When the sum-mer comes a-gain.
clothes they'll give for flow-ers, When the sum-mer comes a-gain.
see we knows our book, Nell, When the sum-mer comes a-gain.

G7   C   G7   C

CHORUS

When the sum-mer comes a - gain_____ and the pret - ty flow'rs are grow-ing, The

sun - shine af - ter rain,_____ the sum-mer breez - es blow-ing;_____ Then to roam a-

-round the coun-try_____ with a girl who's ev - er will - ing_____ I can buy an

she can cry, "Three pots a shil-ling!" When the shil - ling!"